FV

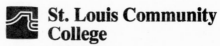

Go! Fight! Win!

Go! Fight! Win!

Cheerleading in American Culture

Mary Ellen Hanson

Bowling Green State University Popular Press
Bowling Green, OH 43403

Copyright © 1995 by Bowling Green State University Popular Press
Cover design by Dumm Art

Library of Congress Cataloging-in-Publication Data
Hanson, Mary Ellen.
    Go! fight! win! : cheerleading in American culture / Mary Ellen
Hanson.
        p.   cm.
    Includes bibliographical references and index.
    ISBN: 0-87972-679-2 (cloth). -- ISBN 0-87972-680-6 (pbk.)
    1. Cheerleading--United States--History. 2. Popular culture--United
States--History.   I. Title.
LB3635.H35   1995
791.6'4'0973--dc20   95-16693
                                                                                CIP

Contents

Illustrations

Following page 74

1. Yell Leader of Indiana University, 1915
2. The 1925 Pep Squad of Trinity University
3. The 1936 cheerleaders at Trinity University
4. The 1937 squad at Trinity University
5. Cheerleaders of Grossmont Union High School, 1944
6. The pom pon squad of Grossmont Union High School, 1945
7. University of Denver ice hockey cheerleaders, 1965
8. Houston Oilers Derrick Dolls cheerleader
9. Houston Oilers Derrick Dolls cheerleader
10. Houston Oilers Derrick Dolls cheerleader
11. Houston Oilers Derrick Dolls cheerleader
12. Greg Evans cartoon
13. Henry Payne editorial cartoon
14. Don Addis cartoon
15. Tom Batiuk cartoon
16. John Louthan cartoon

Acknowledgments

I want to thank my colleagues, friends, and family members for sharing personal anecdotes and clippings from their hometown newspapers—and from tabloids they swear they do not usually read. Thanks also to M. Jane Slaughter, Jane Caputi, Vivian Heyward, and Gary Scharnhorst for reading earlier versions of this manuscript. And special thanks to Carl A. Hanson for cheering me on.

Introduction

Cheerleading is one of the few purely American phenonema,
both in its inception and in its development. We gave the
cheerleaders birth, and we pioneered and nurtured their
growth. In a word, they are ours.
        —Charles Thomas Hatton and Robert W. Hatton[1]

Cheerleading, an American invention with roots in the
institutions of sport and education, has become a staple in
American culture. The cheerleader is a nationally recognized
symbol invested with positive as well as negative cultural values.
Although cheerleading began as a masculine activity, it is now
perceived almost exclusively as a feminized role. This study
examines the evolution and cultural significance of cheerleading
from its origins in the late 1800s to the present.

Over time, cheerleading has become a highly structured
activity shaped by the varied and sometimes conflicting priorities
of educators, entrepreneurs, and mass market media. Cultural
interpretations of the cheerleader's role and image have also been
shaped by these various entities. Is cheerleading a spontaneous
form of youthful expression or a formal mechanism to instill good
behavior among students? Is it a wholesome extracurricular
activity, an exploitative entertainment, a crass marketing tool, or a
challenging athletic sport? Is it the essence of cooperative
teamwork or exhibitionistic individual stardom? Is it exclusionary
and elitist or an egalitarian competitive opportunity? Is it all of
the above?

The Oxford English Dictionary entry for "cheer-leader" cites a
source document which reveals an historical tidbit about an early
practitioner: "cheer-leader (orig. U.S.), one who leads the cheering
on special occasions; also *fig.*; hence cheer-leading . . . 1903 F.D.
Roosevelt *Let.* 26 Oct. (1949) 437, I was one of the three cheer
leaders in the Brown game."[2]

Franklin D. Roosevelt, Harvard, class of 1903, was a typical
cheerleader of his era, a male college student.[3] What began in
nineteenth-century America as an informal expression of male

1

collegiate sports culture has been transformed into a mass phenomenon familiar to anyone who has attended school, watched television, or read a newspaper. Changes in the socioeconomic status and gender roles of participants and changes in the structure, style, and content of cheering have accompanied its transformation to mass culture status and have influenced the sometimes contradictory values ascribed to it.

The cheerleader is an icon, an instantly recognized symbol of youthful prestige, wholesome attractiveness, peer leadership, and popularity. Equally recognized is the cheerleader as symbol of mindless enthusiasm, shallow boosterism, objectified sexuality, and promiscuous availability. How did cheerleading come to represent both the essence of social success and the target of social scorn?

The cheerleader icon is almost always characterized as female, although cheerleading began and flourished for decades as an exclusively masculine enterprise. How did cheerleading, which has been coeducational since the 1920s, become feminized in cultural mythology? This work attempts to address such questions by presenting a broad overview of factors which influenced the metamorphosis of cheerleading from a masculine activity to one perceived almost exclusively as feminine.

The following characterizations of "the cheerleader," written fifty years apart, illustrate how profoundly perceptions changed. In 1924, a *New York Times* editorial speculated how the ancient Greeks would view Stanford University's cheerleaders:

> A contemporary of Pericles, strolling into one of our football stadiums, would . . . delight in those lithe, white-sweatered and flannel-trousered youths in front of the bleachers, their mingled force and grace, their gestures at the same time hieratic and apparently jointless, that accompanied the spelling out of the locomotive cheer. And even an ancient Greek pulse would halt for a moment at that final upward leap of the young body, like a diver into the azure, as the stands thundered out the climactic "Stanford!"[4]

In 1974, an article in *Esquire* noted that

> Cheerleaders are fixed in the popular myth as simple creatures of homespun virtue: ladies of the day, full of

> good cheer. To be one, you need at least two things—
> blondeness, congenital or acquired, and a compulsively
> cute, nonstop bottom. . . . The hair you can always fake,
> the other is up to God. . . . You have to be smart; not too
> smart, just smart enough to master the cheers. You need
> a Good Personality and a Good Reputation.[5]

The heroic, idealized image of the male cheerleader stressed aesthetics as well as skill. This image was replaced by a trivialized image of the female cheerleader which emphasized isolated body parts and minimal ability. While the function of cheerleading did not change essentially in the interval between the above articles, the number of female cheerleaders increased significantly. These very different perceptions of cheerleaders reflect cultural values about gender. Male college students were a recognized social elite in the 1920s. Cheering, perceived as a masculine, collegiate activity, was therefore idealized. By the 1970s, cheering was prevalent in public schools at all socioeconomic levels and it was done primarily by females. Perceived as a feminine subsidiary to masculine athletics, cheering thus became trivialized.

In the 1990s, the picture is somewhat mixed. Professional cheerleading is feminized and eroticized, and, therefore, devalued. School and college cheerleading is coeducational and has become increasingly athletic and competitive, qualities that are generally valued. Contemporary attitudes about the cheerleader reflect both positive and negative stereotypes, but prevailing images generally cast the cheerleader in feminine, devalued terms. Sociologist John Goodger observed:

> People do, after all, bring to sport cultures the
> experience acquired outside them. . . . It would be
> surprising, therefore, if the social principles and
> practices acquired outside sport . . . were not
> represented to some extent in the participants'
> interpretations and definitions of their sport experience.[6]

Historically, cheerleading has presented different sport experiences to male and female participants. These differences are explored in the following chapters.

Webster's Ninth New Collegiate Dictionary defines the cheerleader as "one that calls for and directs organized cheering (as at a football game)."[7] Cheerleading includes the activities of a designated group which leads yells and generally exhorts or encourages verbal crowd participation during athletic events. Cheerleading functions also include the promotion of school spirit, dance and acrobatic entertainment, and competitive cheerleading.

Cheerleading has contributed an often-used metaphor to popular culture: a person who shows enthusiastic support or advocacy for a cause is likely to be labeled a "cheerleader."[8] This appellation can be positive or negative. It is positive when used to characterize an active, principled advocate. It is negative when used to describe an unquestioning booster or a marginal accessory to the more dynamic "player." Positive and negative aspects of this metaphor are applied to males as well as females.

An additional note on terminology is in order for readers who note variations of "pom pon" and "pom pom" in quotations throughout the text. The term for this emblematic prop of the cheerleader's craft is based on "pompon," derived from the French word *pompe,* which refers to ornamental tufts worn on women's or children's hats and shoes or on soldiers' caps and shakos.[9] The cheerleader's pom pon is an extension of the decorative, ceremonial, and militaristic pompon. "Pom pom" occurs often in popular usage, perhaps because it is easier to pronounce. This writer uses "pom pon," following the usage of contemporary cheer instructors and entrepreneurs.

A variety of primary and secondary sources from the late nineteenth century to the present documents the evolution and perception of cheerleading. These sources include magazine and newspaper articles reflecting general interest in this auxiliary aspect of collegiate, scholastic, and professional sport; a body of prescriptive manuals and articles dating from the 1920s to the present; a sampling of college yearbooks from the late nineteenth century to the present; articles from the professional education, medical, and legal literature representing pedagogical and administrative concerns from the 1930s to the present; scholarly articles addressing the popular culture aspects of cheerleading; scholarly monographs on the history and sociology of American sport and education; and a sampling of cartoons, films, advertisements, television programs, juvenile and adult fiction, and news reports which reflect attitudes and values. Additionally, former cheerleaders known to the writer provided anecdotes and insights about their experiences cheering in the 1930s, 1940s,

1960s, 1970s, and 1990s. As a mass phenomenon cheerleading is omnipresent in contemporary journalistic and entertainment media. These sources provide much of the material used to describe and interpret the symbolic significance of cheerleading in American culture today.

Chapter 1 traces the history of cheering from its collegiate beginnings in the late nineteenth century to its spread into secondary schools in the 1900s, and its establishment in elementary and junior high schools by the 1950s. Related activities such as rooter sections, drill teams, and dance teams are described. Women's emergence as cheerleaders in the 1920s and the eventual feminization of scholastic and, to a lesser extent, collegiate cheering are discussed.

Chapter 2 outlines the social context of institutionalization and control of cheerleading. Changing patterns in the social class, age, and race of participants; coeducational participation and the subsequent feminization of cheering at the secondary level; continuing coeducational participation at the collegiate level; and the persistence of gender divisions in youth league and professional cheerleading are described. The selection and regimentation of participants; the professionalization of adult control, including the emergence of coaches and a body of prescriptive literature; and the rise of clinics and camps as training mechanisms are examined. The economics of cheerleading, including fund-raising, financial liability, scholarships, and related businesses such as classes, camps, and "kiddie" gyms are addressed.

Chapter 3 describes the development of cheerleading in professional sports beginning in the 1960s and its relationship with mass media entertainment, promotion, and advertising. Professional cheerleading is compared and contrasted with collegiate and scholastic cheering. The emphasis of pro cheerleading on glamorous sex appeal and dance performance separate from the athletic event is discussed as it has influenced school and college cheering.

Chapter 4 traces the evolution of style and content in cheerleading. Cheering evolved from informal to ritualized and stylized expression. Spontaneous, verbal activity by members of the crowd has given way to highly organized gymnastic and dance performance by specialists. The organization of cheerleaders into "squads" and "teams," adoption of uniforms, and increased demands for physical conditioning and extensive practice, all signify greater formality in the cheerleader's role. Changes in the style of performance have also occurred. The early direct relationship between cheerleaders and game spectators has evolved to include less direct interaction with crowds and more emphasis on stunts which are independent of the athletic events taking place on the field. The ultimate extension of this tendency is evident in the rise of state, national, and international contests which define cheerleading as a competitive activity in its own right. Collegiate and scholastic cheerleading, originally an adjunct to sport events, is increasingly defined as a sport itself. A parallel trend is an increased emphasis on cheerleading as entertainment related to, or separated from, the athletic event at which it occurs. Collegiate song girls and drill teams which emerged in the 1940s influenced the trend toward cheerleader dance groups in professional sports in the 1970s.

Chapter 5 addresses the meanings, values, and symbolism associated with cheerleading in American culture. The cheerleader as icon reflects cultural values about youth, sports, sex, morality, success, and celebrity. The cheerleader embodies many positive as well as negative stereotypes: wholesomeness vs. the sexual sell; the peppy, perky, and popular student vs. the mindless booster or aggressive hypester; the epitome of youthful success or the personification of the bimbo; Big Man on Campus or peripheral accessory. The acceptance of these images is evident in their proliferation throughout American culture. Examples of these themes are described. The emotional importance, both trivial and tragic, which some Americans attach to cheerleading is exemplified in the notorious Cheerleader Hit Mom case which made national news in 1991 and is currently scheduled for retrial, based on an appeals court review in 1994.

There are many different avenues to investigate cheerleading. Folkloric analysis of the texts of specific cheers could examine style, topic, imagery, and geographic patterns of distribution and use. Systematic oral histories of cheerleaders, coaches, players, and administrators could document individual experiences by gender, socioeconomic status, region, type of school, and time period. Content analysis of popular media could trace the portrayal of cheerleaders in a variety of contexts. Comparisons between juvenile and adult literature, movies and television, drama and commercials, or editorial cartoons and comic strips are a few of many possibilities. Detailed analysis of the considerable body of prescriptive manuals, articles, and instructional videos could illustrate changes (and continuity) in the rhetoric and rationale of cheerleading. These are some aspects of the institution of cheerleading which could be examined in more detail. The present study serves as an introduction to stimulate awareness of what cheerleading tells us about ourselves and our culture. E. Ann Kaplan, discussing the study of popular culture, noted: "It's important to read back from the phenomenon its values, its ideas, its forms, its modes, and to theorize about its impact, what it means that [we] are consuming it daily."[10]

Although hundreds of published sources treat various aspects of cheerleading, there has not been a detailed overview of its historical development and cultural significance. The present work is intended to provide an initial synthesis as a basis for additional study and continuing interpretation.

1

Collegiate and Scholastic Beginnings

Two images sum up contemporary popular understanding of the term "cheerleader." She is a wholesome Chosen One from our high school's pantheon of popularity or she is a scantily clad dancer, gyrating on-camera at professional football games. The cheerleader is nearly always seen as female, and cheerleading is regarded as a feminine activity. The act of leading cheers for one's team, however, began as a purely masculine enterprise. To understand this transformation, it is necessary to examine the development of cheerleading from the college playing field to the professional franchise.

The American phenomenon of cheerleading, which today involves all age groups and social strata in venues as diverse as network television and neighborhood recreation leagues, originated within the elite confines of nineteenth-century collegiate life. Only an estimated two percent of American youth between eighteen and twenty-one years of age attended college in the early 1800s, and that small group was white, male, and predominantly of British descent.[1]

In reaction to the often severely harsh authority exerted by faculty in the post-Revolutionary War era, college students sometimes rioted, assaulted teachers, and burned campus buildings. As a milder gesture of independence, students developed their own social and recreational activities outside of faculty control.[2] Prior to the Civil War, interclass and intramural sports provided informal competition, but intercollegiate contests soon dominated student interest. Gregory Sojka provides a chronology of significant events: August 3, 1852—The first intercollegiate athletic contest, a crew match between Harvard and Yale clubs. July 1, 1859—The first intercollegiate baseball game. Amherst defeated Williams. November 6, 1869—The first intercollegiate football game. Rutgers defeated Princeton.[3]

Participation in intercollegiate athletics intensified institutional identity and enabled students to define heroic personal identities for themselves. Interschool rivalries incited "intense fighting spirit and loyalty to the college among students. The rows of athletes gathered for team pictures offer carefully posed self-presentations of virility and newly acquired adulthood."[4] Students were the organizers of early college athletics, forming teams and setting rules which governed intercollegiate play in the 1870s. With growing numbers of college alumni and increased community interest in the spectacles offered, college athletics attracted audiences beyond the primary groups of male undergraduate students which had developed the games for their own amusement.

The lack of official institutional identification with athletics can be inferred from student activities listed in college catalogs. Grace Stark surveyed catalogs from the 1840s to the 1880s. Although colleges described a variety of student pastimes from gardening to music, during this period of growing student involvement in collegiate sport, there is no mention of athletics.[5]

Collegiate Volunteers

Student interest in intercollegiate athletic contests manifested itself in spectatorship and social events related to the games. It was not possible for all interested members of the male student body to play on the elite baseball or football teams, but travel to games in other cities and attendance during the contests were ways to show loyalty and to participate vicariously. Cheering during games began as an informal, sporadic activity. A young man in the crowd would occasionally step out and urge fellow male students to yell. Some of the early unofficial cheerleaders were injured or substitute players "who left the bench in order to lead the spectators in a spontaneous cheer."[6] Early contests took place on playing fields with little or no seating. Crowds stood around the edge of the playing area close to the action of the game. As attendance grew and large stadiums were constructed, spectators were distanced from the playing field and less able to conduct spontaneous commentary audible to players in the course of the game.

Organized cheering evolved as a way to intensify spectator involvement within the increasingly structured context of formal athletic competition. As early as the 1869 Princeton-Rutgers football game, "some Nassau Hall residents let fly with a throaty 'Siss, boom, Ahhh!' . . . rocket cheer."[7] Cheering by self-appointed groups was one way to stimulate verbal participation by the larger crowd. If sufficiently inspired, spectators might also toss "bowlers, toppers and ladies' handkerchiefs" onto the field.[8] The systemization of cheering paralleled systemization in the nature of the games played on the field. In 1905 Ralph Paine compared the "primitive pastime" of English rugby, introduced at Yale and Harvard thirty years earlier, with its elaborate descendant, American-style football, characterized by "military strategy," extended spring training, padded and armored uniforms, tackling dummies, training-tables, coaches, and "a small army of trainers and attendants."[9] By the turn of the century the competitive stakes were considerable. As Paine noted: "The rewards of victory before thirty thousand raving spectators, the honor of winning a championship, and the newspaper notoriety which magnifies the feat, breed in coaches and players a feverish desire to win."[10] The "feverish desire to win" was also reflected in those "raving spectators," primarily male students, whose cheering might inspire the home team and intimidate the opposition.

During the late 1800s and early 1900s cheering was often led by individual male volunteers who would stand in front of the crowd and urge spectators to yell. An 1897 photograph showing a Stanford student as he leads men in the grandstand to cheer during a football game is similar to a photograph, c. 1905, captioned "A cheering faction and its leader at an American championship game."[11] Both leaders are wearing suits and derby hats, as are most of the spectators. The leaders stand at ground level with their backs to the field, waving their arms and exhorting the crowd.

Yell Leaders

By the 1890s some colleges had a formally designated "cheer leader" who might also be known as a "rooter king," "yell leader," "yell king," "yell master," or "yell marshall." One of the first designated yell marshalls was Johnny Campbell, at the University of Minnesota in 1898.[12] As a graduate, Campbell continued to lead a group in the stands at Minnesota football games for forty years.[13] While most yell leaders were students, Arturo Gonzales notes that "USC's first cheerleader was a frock-coated faculty professor."[14]

By the early twentieth century organized cheering and cheerleaders were sufficiently institutionalized to inspire both detractors and defenders. In a 1911 article, *The Nation* tweaked Harvard's President A. Lawrence Lowell for his "audacity to pour ridicule upon sacred undergraduate traditions." Lowell, addressing a convention of music teachers, had criticized "organized cheering as being nearly the worst means of expressing emotion ever invented." *The Nation* countered that the essence of college loyalty "consists in going off to an intercollegiate contest in an immense *claque* to yell and sing at the word of command." The article defended the role of the cheerleader in extravagant terms:

> The reputation of having been a valiant "cheer-leader" is one of the most valuable things a boy can take away from college. As a title to promotion in professional or public life, it ranks hardly second to that of having been a quarter-back.[15]

This tongue-in-cheek editorial alluded to the prestige accorded collegiate sports heroes and other student leaders. A widely accepted rationale for collegiate athletics was its value in preparing male students for the rigors of competitive business life. Yell leaders were charismatic, highly visible, solo performers who emerged or were selected because of their popularity, personality, or perceived leadership abilities. Both quarterback and cheerleader served as symbols of undergraduate leadership which would translate into professional success in adult life.

In the late nineteenth century colleges brought athletics "into the curriculum."[16] By hiring professional coaches as faculty members, establishing leagues, scheduling play, paying scholarships, and supervising the activities of marching bands and yell leaders, the schools assumed formal control over diversions which the students had once organized outside college authority. As college football became "an immense spectacle and winning teams the objects of devotion," college authorities found that sports helped to curb unruly student behavior and "provided a focus for alumni loyalty" which included financial gifts to the schools.[17]

Institutional approval of increasingly competitive athletics was not universal. Educators such as Reed College's William T. Foster editorialized against "athletics for business" (varsity sports) in favor of "athletics for everybody" (intramurals). In 1915 Foster decried the money colleges spent for "trainers, coaches, banners . . . training tables, railroad fares . . . costly uniforms . . . advertising, grand-stands, brass bands and rallies."[18] These trappings of big-time collegiate athletics, including rallies and organized cheering, were commonplace by the early 1900s.

Nineteenth-century collegiate culture, created by students, evolved from hooliganism to interest in athletic and social pursuits. Student-initiated teams, clubs, and societies became formalized parts of college life by the early twentieth century. W.H. Cowley, in 1926, characterized the domestication of the once-rowdy undergraduate:

> The eagerness which once went into defying authority and chastising freshmen now goes largely into the great organizations of student life. . . . [I]nstead of rough and roaring terrorists, the college is composed of athletes . . . editors, managers, amateur actors, and the less ambitious undergraduates who do little except cheer at the college's athletic encounters. The defiant . . . fire-eater has gone, and in his place has come the well dressed, well mannered (except perhaps at football games) undergraduate, sometimes contemptuously referred to as the Rah Rah Boy.[19]

In the 1920s the Rah Rah Boy symbolized a carefree undergraduate experience which emphasized social life over academic pursuits. The Rah Rah Boy was likely to be a spectator in contrast to the cheerleader on the field who was perceived as a leader, a Big Man on Campus. In 1924 *Literary Digest* quoted Chicago baseball celebrity "Hughie" Fullerton, who observed that "the position of cheer-leader nowadays is fraught with great responsibility and rated as a high honor, so much so that in many colleges competitions and examinations are held to select the cheer-leaders."[20]

Just as elite athletes were singled out to compete for the college, cheerleaders representing the college were now selected for their tumbling skills and extroverted personalities. Cheerleaders were chosen by various groups, including faculty committees, physical education departments, or the student body. Preliminary training sessions and competition in the form of "tryouts" were part of the selection process by the 1920s. Big-time athletics now required more than a casual volunteer, and the status of a formally selected yell leader rose accordingly.

The popularity of college athletics extended beyond the campus to civic and regional involvement. Urbanization, mass transit, the emergence of mass print and radio media, and increased leisure time fostered spectatorship as a means of affiliation and entertainment. Game crowds grew from hundreds to thousands. Collegiate sports facilities responded to civic demand. Paula Fass observes, "The twenties saw a veritable orgy of stadium-building . . . [symbolic] of a football mania perhaps never equaled in modern college history."[21]

Uniforms, consisting of slacks and sweaters in school colors, and the use of megaphones became routine for yell leaders of this era. By the 1920s some colleges began to use multiple cheerleaders who performed synchronized yells and acrobatics. In 1924 Princeton and Yale each had three male cheerleaders, as did Baylor by 1927.[22] These changes may have resulted from the logistical problem of one person trying to be visible and to mobilize thousands of spectators in a large stadium.

Evidence that organized cheering was widespread in American colleges by the 1920s is demonstrated in the 1927 publication, *Just Yells: A Guide for Cheer Leaders*, which lists specific cheers from 143 colleges and universities, alphabetically by school. Public, private, elite, state, small, and large institutions from all regions of the country are represented. The compilers noted, "There has been for some time a considerable demand for a book of cheers. This book is an attempt to supply that demand."[23] Cheers from high schools are also included in *Just Yells*, indicating concomitant development of cheering at the scholastic level.

Flash Card Rooter Sections

The flash card, another innovation in systematized college cheering, presented visual as well as audible impact in large outdoor arenas. While several California schools, including Stanford, claim to have invented the use of flash cards, "it is believed to have first taken place, however primitively, on the occasion of the Yale Bowl Dedication Day of 1914."[24] Lindley Bothwell is credited with developing the first large-scale flash-card section while he was yell king at the University of Southern California, from 1920 to 1923.[25] Under his guidance, USC epitomized this form of cheering with a 2,500-man section trained, on signal, to form letters and designs with large flash cards. Seated in tight formation in the stands, cheering section members were highly regimented and dressed uniformly in white shirts, bow ties, and bellhop-style caps. In 1923 Bothwell took the practice to Oregon State University.

In 1938 *Scholastic Magazine* noted that "the California cheering sections are in a class by themselves. But the weather has a lot to do with it," since the snow and winds in eastern and mid-western climates "make shirtsleeves and flash cards impractical."[26] Flash-card sections did become popular at other schools. Cheerleading instructor Newt Loken, writing in 1945, observed that USC, the University of California at Los Angeles (UCLA), and the U.S. Naval Academy were "famed for the dexterity of their . . . flash-card stunts."[27]

The phenomenon of organized cheering was not limited to athletic contests and rallies. Student bodies, assembled for academic convocations, were sometimes led in cheers honoring professors and speakers as a preliminary to the formal program. Foreign awareness of this aspect of cheering is exemplified by a 1929 article in the London *Times Educational Supplement*. The *Times* correspondent contrasts the individualized verbal rowdiness typical in British university halls with the "standardized," "manipulated" yells of American students: "Everybody knows that the Americans are super-organizers, so no one need be surprised that students' ebullitions . . . are organized to a fine point." This behavior was attributed to the yell leader, a "trained standardizer" who "sets himself wittingly to stir up certain emotions and to guide them into channels that he chooses. . . . [H]is power is limited, but within its range that power is great."[28]

Collegiate Women Cheerleaders

The exact date when women began participating as cheerleaders at the college level is not known, but the 1920s appear to have been the transitional period. The pattern of women's involvement at Trinity University, San Antonio, Texas, may be typical. In 1923 Trinity had a pep squad of 15 men and 15 women, with one man designated as Yell Leader. In 1925 the squad had 12 men and 22 women, with one woman designated as Cheer Leader, and one man as Assistant Cheer Leader. By 1929 the squad consisted of 29 men and 28 women, with a male Cheer Leader and three Assistant Cheer Leaders, two female and one male. The large group pattern continued until 1936, when three cheerleaders were featured, a female and two male assistants. Yearbook photos show the Trinity pep squads of the 1920s marching on playing fields and in parades and posed in formal "glee club" formations. From the 1930s on, the smaller cheerleader groups are posed in more athletic style on the field, kneeling, jumping, and cheering with megaphones.[29] Women emerged as leaders of the larger pep clubs and, from those conspicuous roles, made the transition to the smaller cheerleader squads which performed on the sidelines.

Female cheerleaders did meet some early resistance from their male colleagues. A 1939 article in *Time* profiling Gamma Sigma, the national college cheerleaders' fraternity, reported that "though some of the most versatile cheerleaders at Southern colleges (notably Alabama and Tennessee) are dimple-kneed co-eds, girls are not eligible for the All-America squad."[30] Young women were excluded from the cheerleader All-America seven (the size of most college squads of the era) chosen annually by Gamma Sigma and sports journalists. *Time* quoted Gamma Sigma president Andrew Ritter of the University of Michigan: "Every year there is a campaign to take them in, but every year we keep them out." *Time*'s editorial policy was less restrictive; one of the photographs illustrating the article shows a Tennessee cheerleader, Wilma Rogers, jumping energetically alongside a male squad member.[31]

Women students were excluded from the private, all-male colleges where student-led athletics first developed, but the proliferation of state-supported and land-grant institutions opened enrollment to females during the period that big-time collegiate athletics began to emerge. Iowa admitted women in 1855; Wisconsin in 1867; Kansas, Indiana, and Minnesota in 1869; Missouri, Michigan, and California in 1870.[32] Horowitz notes that as late as the turn of the century, male students on some coeducational campuses sought to maintain traditional male college life:

> They pushed the women students aside, barring them from any place where they might serve as troubling reminders that Cornell was not Yale. . . . Women were kept out of key activities on campus: student government, the newspaper, honor societies, athletics. . . . In time, coeds would find a new source of prestige, but this awaited changing sexual codes and the discovery by college men that college women could be amusing.[33]

The "new source of prestige" accorded to college women emerged from the development of dating as conspicuous competition. In contests "of beauty and personality" female students achieved status by associating with popular male students. The status of male students was, in turn, enhanced by association with attractive coeds. By the 1920s "the conventional college woman was becoming the consort of the college man."[34] This social competition occurred in the context of fraternity and sorority control. Fraternities, already "conspicuous in campus life by the 1890s," were, by the 1920s, "at the center of college life."[35] Just as athletics were brought into the curriculum, college administrators endorsed fraternities as organizations "useful in the supervision and control of students."[36] With administrative concurrence the fraternities took increasing control of extra-curricular activities, defining their content and selecting the student leaders who would preside over them.

Women's participation as collegiate cheerleaders may have resulted from factors which developed on campus in the 1920s: fraternity and sorority dominance in student culture, and the increasing emphasis on physical attractiveness and its conspicuous display as a value in coeducational student social life. Campus attitudes reflected changing cultural values. As noted by John D'Emilio and Estelle Freedman:

> The new positive value attributed to the erotic, the growing autonomy of youth, the association of sex with commercialized leisure and self-expression, the pursuit of love, the visibility of the erotic in popular culture, the social interaction of men and women in public, the legitimization of female interest in the sexual: all of these were to be seen in America in the twenties.[37]

By the 1920s phenomena such as beauty pageants and motion pictures emphasized female display as mass entertainment. The acceptance of female "sex appeal" in advertising and entertainment could easily have extended to the spectacle of collegiate football.

While women were established as collegiate cheerleaders by the 1930s, in the late 1920s the cheerleader or yell leader was still defined in masculine terms. Two of the earliest manuals on cheerleading, both published in 1927, refer exclusively to the "man," "chap," and "fellow" who is, or aspires to be, cheer-leader.[38] This perception of gender role exclusivity began to break down in the 1930s and by the 1940s collegiate cheering squads could be coeducational, all men, or all women. Cheerleading manuals published in 1945 and 1948 contain photographs of college teams in each configuration.[39] It is likely that the mid-1940s war-time mobilization of male college students offered additional opportunities for women to serve as cheerleaders.

Men and women have continued to cheer at the college level to the present, although some institutions were slow to permit women on their squads. The *New York Times* reported in 1975 that the University of Michigan ended "a 94-year-old tradition" when it fielded a coeducational cheerleading squad and "pom-pom girls joined the previously all-male contingent, mostly gymnasts and divers."[40] The story implies that the women were decorative additions to a team of athletic male cheerleaders.

Song Girls

Song girls, an early form of feminized cheering, began at the college level and served as prototype for the dance troupes now identified with professional sports. Song girls appeared as early as 1929 at UCLA football games. At a time when "yell leaders were always fellas . . . it was traditional to sing a song with the band, so the girls would lead the singing and wave the pompoms."[41] The song girls incorporated dance routines by the 1950s and eventually dropped singing altogether. Dance groups are now fixtures at school, college, and professional games.

By the 1950s women were established in two varieties of collegiate cheering, standard cheerleading squads and dance-oriented groups. A 1959 *Life* magazine profile featured the five-member UCLA Song Girls, who did dance routines with pom pons to band numbers played during games, and the Michigan State six-man, six-woman cheerleader squad, known for its "rigorous acrobatics" and 200 different athletic stunts.[42] Coeducational cheerleading teams persist at the college level, as do all-female dance groups. Both types of cheering represent a transition from the directly supportive role of the individual yell leader to an auxiliary entertainment role enhancing the pageantry of an athletic event.

School Cheerleaders

At the secondary school level, the development of a student activity culture and the institutionalization of athletics paralleled the collegiate experience. Prior to the twentieth century only a small percentage of American youth attended high school, since high school was preparatory to an elite college education. Early in the twentieth century child labor laws and rising age limits for compulsory school attendance made secondary school a mass experience. Fass notes, "By the early 1930s, 60 percent of America's youths of high-school age were in school."[43] As high school attendance rose, professional educators redefined the fundamental mission of secondary schooling.

In 1893 the Committee of Ten, chaired by Harvard's president, Charles W. Eliot, advocated a classically oriented curriculum of "Greek, Latin, mathematics, oratory, and writing" to prepare students for higher education. In contrast, a committee of the National Education Association published *The Cardinal Principles of Secondary Education* in 1917. Reflecting recognition that high schools served many lower- and middle-class students who would not go on to college, the *Principles* outlined goals of the comprehensive high school which would "prepare the students for vocations and teach them the social values essential for coping with modern life."[44] The high school would inculcate "social cohesion" in ethnically diverse students by their participation in "common activities . . . such as athletic games, social activities, and the government of the school."[45]

Given their emphasis on educating for social values, high school authorities had strong impetus to direct all aspects of student life, including athletics. As with collegiate competition, high school officials assumed control over activities originated by students:

> High school sport had begun in the nineteenth century
> at the initiative of the students themselves; students had
> formed the first athletic organizations, scheduled the
> first games, managed the finances, and hired seasonal
> coaches. By the 1890s, the rage for football in the larger
> high schools equalled or surpassed that of the colleges.[46]

In the first two decades of the twentieth century, high school educators formed state-wide interscholastic athletic organizations to regulate competition.[47] Just as the colleges had done, high schools brought athletics and related student activities into the curriculum.

Adult intervention was thorough. When Ethel Percy Andrus became principal at Lincoln High School, Los Angeles, in 1916, she found a school "in the cellar" athletically, with low attendance at football games and a "rooting section of twenty" out of its 1,200 students. She organized school assemblies in which students and players instructed fellow students in the rules and tactics of football, "first at the blackboard and then on the field with a megaphone." Once the game was understood, additional assemblies were held to teach Lincoln students "the yells." Andrus reported in the 1917 *National Education Association Proceedings and Addresses*: "Our first.real game found most of the Lincolnites on the bleachers rooting so vigorously that [Lincoln] tied the score with [a] team which seemingly had entirely outclast [*sic*] them."[48] Lincoln's football fortunes continued to improve. Andrus also directed school faculty to secretly "adopt" each of the fifty football players and by "spurring, inspiration, and perhaps nagging" encourage them to make their grades.

Imitating collegiate athletics, the secondary schools fielded yell leaders, cheerleaders, marching bands, and rooter sections. Unlike the colleges, public high schools sponsored girls' athletics, which also received cheerleader support. Gertrude Morrison's 1914 young adult novel, *The Girls of Central High at Basketball*, describes boys leading cheers for the girls' team.[49] It is not known when girls first served as school cheerleaders, but their presence was noted in the popular press by the 1920s. *Literary Digest* quoted Ohio's football coach in 1924:

> We have had a great run of girl cheer-leaders in high schools in this State. As I have observed, these one-half dozen girls controlled high-school audiences better than boys. I do not believe this would be the case in college. . . . [Most of these girls] are fine-looking, bobbed-haired, rhythmic, well-formed individuals who are just outstanding physical girls. They seem to have a better sense of rhythm than most boys, and get splendid results by occasional intensity of action.[50]

While this *Literary Digest* piece emphasizes male college cheerleaders in pictures and text, it includes one photograph of high school girls cheering. The caption reads in part: "This aviating sextet have just reached the crescendo of a complicated yell for 'Morris High's' football team at the goal posts."[51] Shown in mid-leap, the girls wear uniforms consisting of heavy sweaters with a large "M" emblem, ankle-length wool pleated skirts, and white oxfords. They approximate the masculine model both in action and in dress.

Girl cheerleaders were still a novelty in the 1920s as scholastic cheering continued to emulate the college pattern. York's 1927 manual, which addresses high school as well as college cheering, mentions a scholastic boy-girl "rooter group" in passing, but the text and illustrations feature collegiate males. In 1928, *World Review* reprinted an article from *American Boy* magazine indicative of the masculine presence in collegiate cheering and its influence on scholastic cheering. Directed to "everyone who is interested in high school cheering," it stated:

> You're now aboard the Pep Special, and you're going
> . . . to chat with the Big Time cheer leaders, the duck-
> trousered, jersied, agile, smiling Pep Producers of
> Washington, Illinois, Alabama, Princeton, Minnesota,
> Missouri, Southern California, and all points in every
> direction.[52]

In the article college men at each school describe their practice regimens and give pointers on how they perform their signature school cheers.

Girls continued to participate as high school cheerleaders in the 1930s. While some educators expressed concern that cheering would adversely affect a girl's behavior or character, popular sentiment considered it prestigious. The heroine of a 1934 young adult novel dreams of being "eligible for the highest honor for girls in high school, the much coveted position of cheer leader."[53] In 1938 educator John Gach summarized "The Case For and Against Girl Cheerleaders," concluding that girls should be allowed to cheer. Arguments against girls included their inability to do acrobatic stunts and concerns that they would develop harsh voices, unladylike "smart-alecky" conduct, and excessive conceit. Gach countered that these problems could be avoided in girls (and boys) with proper adult coaching and supervision. Gach also offered arguments in favor of girl cheerleaders:

> Girls are more magnetic in appearance and will become
> the center of attention for the crowd and the leading of
> cheers will, therefore, be easy. . . . Inasmuch as football
> and other interscholastic avenues are not open to girls,
> the prospect of leading cheers is an opportunity to add

something to the usually too restricted program of extra-curricular activities for girls.[54]

Since cheerleading was viewed as a masculine activity, objections to girls' participation were expressed in terms of gender-appropriate behavior. Girls were thought to be incapable of doing athletic stunts; athleticism was seen as a masculine role. If girls did perform as cheerleaders, they would become mannish. Gach's well-intentioned rationale defined girls' cheerleading in acceptably feminine terms: girls, it was assumed, could lead a crowd to cheer because they were attractive. Boys, it was assumed, could lead cheers because they were aggressive and athletic.

Scholastic cheering imitated the forms of collegiate cheering, such as rooter sections, but invested them with socializing and character-building functions beyond their college models. Early college cheerleaders sought to maximize and focus audience noise to gain an emotional advantage for the team on the field. Attendant values of entertainment and pageantry were later outgrowths of the evolving spectacle of college games. When a secondary school adopted a college-style flash-card rooter section, it was likely to transform it into a mechanism of socialization and instruction for the participating students. The Pepnocrats of Connersville (Indiana) High School typified the scholastic approach. In 1937 Connersville's assistant athletic director was concerned about booing, paper throwing, and "constant din during the shooting of fouls" at basketball games. He organized a cheering section of 150 boys and girls "to spread the gospel of good sportsmanship among the students [and] the public as well."[55] Dressed in white shirts and red bellhop caps and equipped with megaphones and large flash cards, the Pepnocrats performed songs, cheers, and card designs during games. Their slogan, "We don't boo—Do you?," typified the behavior they sought to promote. Additionally, a subcommittee of Pepnocrats was appointed as a court "to try cases of [unsportsmanlike] conduct by students."[56] Colleges allowed students to define the content of extracurricular life and to control their own behavior via the social influence of student fraternities. At the scholastic level, in contrast, the adult goal of shaping student values transformed extracurricular activities into formal pedagogical and disciplinary tools.

Girls and boys continued to perform as scholastic cheerleaders in the 1940s, in coeducational as well as same-sex groups. Girls were accepted as leaders and in one instance received national recognition for innovation. In 1941 *Life* profiled three senior girls from the Whiting (Indiana) High School who devised "rhythm-nastics," a lively style of cheering combining words, gymnastics, and popular contemporary dance. Joyce Wargo, Gloria Huenger, and Nancy Johnson are shown doing cheers which "reveal their familiarity with conga, rumba, trucking and shag." *Life's* hyperbole reveals a rationale for women cheerleaders based on sex appeal:

> To anyone acquainted with mass psychology the superiority of girls over boys in the delicate art of cheerleading is axiomatic. Yet it is only lately, perhaps because of the world's belated acceptance of coeducation, that the girl cheerleader has bounced into her own.[57]

The pictorial features action shots of the three girls jumping, kicking, and jiving through a cheer. Their uniforms are emblem sweaters, full, knee-length skirts, and saddle shoes. *Life* clucks approvingly, "If they have a failing it is that grandstands more often watch them than the players giving their all for Whiting on the field of combat."[58]

Dance was considered appropriate for girl cheerleaders, but some concern continued over girls' participation in acrobatic stunts. Lawrence Brings's 1944 manual, *School Yells*, which shows photographs of coeducational and same-sex squads, quotes an Easton (Pennsylvania) High School educator who wanted to use "as much tumbling as possible," but felt constrained: "Such actions as cartwheels, forward and backward rolls, flips, head and hand stands, and diving, are about all we can use now, for the trend is more and more toward girls."[59] The implication is that girls could do basic tumbling, but not the more advanced stunts. Newt Loken and Otis Dypwick's 1945 manual shows equal numbers of male and female cheerleaders, but males are used in the formal sequence shots which illustrate acrobatics. Most of the photographs of female cheerleaders are informal action shots taken during games. There is an apparent gender division between instructional and candid illustrations.

In the 1940s, despite reservations about their athleticism—and perhaps because of continued emphasis on female display as an entertainment value—girls became cheerleaders at the scholastic level in greater numbers. They had more opportunities, since over 30,000 American high schools and colleges had cheerleaders by the mid-1940s.[60] Boys and girls continued to lead cheers in the 1950s, but a gradual feminization of the activity was occurring. A 1955 overview of scholastic cheering programs highlighted two trends: a differentiation between "true cheerleading as such and the elaborate pep-routine, half-time demonstration type of activity," and the prevalence of girls.[61] This article noted that in large schools "occasionally boys as well as girls are included," but that in smaller schools "boys can usually find their place in the athletic program, and cheerleading is likely to remain solely a feminine occupation."[62]

By the 1950s cheerleading had spread to junior high and elementary schools. *Life*, in 1954, profiled an aspiring child model who was an eighth-grade cheerleader at Dalton School in New York City.[63] In 1958 Harold Hainfeld described how sixth- through eighth-grade girls in Union City, New Jersey, formed cheering squads in support of a boys' elementary school basketball league sponsored by the Board of Education. The program, which began circa 1953, included girls' cheering squads in each school which fielded a boys' basketball team. "Varsity" girls in seventh and eighth grade made their own costumes and attended weekly practice sessions. One school modeled its costumes on a cowgirl theme similar to that worn by the Kilgore College Rangerettes, a Texas drill team featured in the Cotton Bowl halftime show televised in 1958. "Junior varsity" sixth-grade girls were coached by the varsity girls and promoted to varsity level when they advanced to seventh grade. Hainfeld observed that "almost all [girls in the program] go on to the high school pep activities as members of the drill squad, majorettes, or as cheerleaders."[64] In the 1950s some secondary school educators defined gender-appropriate activities as sports for boys and cheerleading (and sewing) for girls. A masculine activity in the 1800s, which was transitional in the 1920s and 1930s, by the 1950s had become primarily a feminine experience. As the New Jersey program indicates, school control of student life now extended to the extracurricular activities of the elementary school.

Outside the schools, additional structures developed which influenced cheerleading at the secondary level. In the 1961 edition of his cheerleading manual Newt Loken noted several developments of the 1950s: cheerleading clinics and camps run by entrepreneurs such as Lawrence Herkimer; the formation of the

National Cheerleaders Association which published a quarterly, *The Megaphone*; and the formation of the United States Cheerleaders Association and the American Cheerleaders Association.[65] These workshops and publications provided additional instruction to cheerleaders, their coaches, and their advisors. While the schools continued to exercise administrative control over cheerleading, the proliferation of camps and clinics influenced cheering style, technique, and content.

School cheerleading now entailed considerable training, practice, supervision, and discipline. Loken compared the cheerleading squad to an athletic team:

> The faculty sponsor of the cheerleading squad is its "coach," and a good coach is interested in and trained in his sport. The head cheerleader corresponds to the athletic team captain and is responsible for the actions of the squad on the field. . . . A football team strives for perfection through lots of practice. The successful cheerleading squad must do likewise. . . . Football players must win their positions, and so should cheerleaders.[66]

Loken makes a case for symbolically comparing the structure of cheering to the structure of a sport, but he does not define the content of cheering as a sport in itself. These arguments would come later, as strength and gymnastic skills required for cheerleading increased in caliber, and as separate cheerleading competitions emerged.

Cheerleading, song leading, and precision drill teams continue to the present. While each activity has stylistic elements in common, functions are specialized and are usually performed by separate groups. Cheerleading continues to be coeducational, while song-leading (dance) teams and drill teams are defined as feminine activities. Marylou and Ron Humphrey's 1970 manual, *Cheerleading and Song Leading*, treats both forms of cheering and is careful to distinguish functions and participants:

> Both boys and girls make good cheerleaders. Many schools prefer boys, but combination boy-girl teams and all-girl teams are popular too. . . . [Their] main job is to control and direct the students. They develop the cheer routines and lead the students in cheering. Song leaders

are always girls. . . . [Their] primary purpose is to
perform during the singing of school songs and to
entertain the students with special routines during
pauses in game activity.[67]

The authors state that cheerleading and song leading "to be
done properly, should not be combined." They recommend
separate teams but advise schools that can field only one team to
"spend the greater part of your time on cheerleading."[68] Scholastic
song-leading groups imitated the collegiate model popularized by
UCLA in the 1950s. The California influence is alluded to in *The
Encyclopedia of Cheerleading,* which notes that "song girl" is a West
Coast term and that "pom pon girl" is the equivalent used "east
of Death Valley."[69]

Drill teams and pom pon squads provided opportunities for
many girls to participate. Both groups perform precision march
routines, the latter using large pom pons for increased visual
effect. The drill teams, with several dozen members, enabled more
girls to participate than did the limited size of cheerleading
squads. However, drill teams, which required tryouts or
competitive selection similar to cheerleading, were more restrictive
than the early pep and rooter clubs which any interested student
could join.

Orlino Castro's 1975 photographic documentary follows the
pom pon squad of Robert Peary High School, Rockville,
Maryland, during one year of training and competition. Castro
elaborates on the differences between cheerleading and drill
teams: "The cheerleaders deal with the crowd more . . . for they
have to command. Properly trained cheerleaders can rally
support and interest from the crowd under the most adverse
conditions."[70] In contrast, the drill team's "precision marches and
turns," its "simultaneous snaps," and "tricky transitions from one
formation to another" have to be watched as a performance "by
themselves and in their entirety."[71]

Randy Neil estimated in 1975 that "more than 500,000
students from grade school through college are active cheerleaders," and that "95 percent of America's cheerleaders are
female."[72] He acknowledged that "in recent years, the male
contingent in pep and spirit has somewhat lost out" and to
counter this trend, "thousands of high schools are now
encouraging male students to try out for cheerleading."[73] Neil
editorialized against rules which excluded boys from cheering

squads and pep clubs. In 1978 Charles and Robert Hatton noted that "the almost total dominance of high school cheerleading by girls has given the art a feminine quality, thereby excluding . . . athletically inclined boys, who would be a real asset."[74]

Scholastic cheerleading continued to be a predominantly feminine activity into the 1980s, although collegiate cheering in the same period remained coeducational. Tradition was probably the main factor in the continued involvement of men at the college level. Men constituted the majority of college students during the emergence of big-time collegiate athletics. Male students invented the form, which became identified with "the college man." College cheerleading, however, also sustained feminized forms of cheering represented by song girls and "dimple-kneed coeds." Since few athletic activities were open to girls prior to the 1970s, the more feminine forms of cheering took hold in secondary schools. In one hundred years' time cheerleading had changed from an exclusively masculine role to an activity perceived as primarily feminine.

2

Institutionalization and Commercialization in School, Community, and College Cheerleading

> Cheerleading is no different from Little League baseball or college athletics. . . . It's a great performance opportunity for students. But then the adults get involved, and they squeeze the spontaneity out of it, so that it doesn't seem extracurricular anymore.
>
> —Joe Paul, dean of student development and cheerleader administrator, University of Southern Mississippi[1]

By the 1920s college cheerleading had evolved from informal, spectator demonstrations to a formal, extracurricular activity. Public secondary schools, using extracurricular activities as pedagogical devices, took the institutionalization of cheerleading further, structuring all aspects of selection, conduct, training, and supervision. Formalization at school, community, and college levels was reinforced by a cheerleading industry which developed to promote standards, products, and services. Under adult control, cheerleading became both a didactic tool and a profitable enterprise.

The Structured Experience

Under adult supervision, cheerleading in schools, colleges, and community programs became a highly structured activity. Formal mechanisms developed to determine who would cheer, how they would learn to cheer, how they would behave, and how they would represent their respective institutions. In defining cheerleading as an extracurricular activity, educators invested it with educational and social value. Participants would learn and demonstrate good sportsmanship, discipline, cooperation, and leadership. As student leaders and highly visible ambassadors for their schools, cheerleaders would exemplify acceptable social and

29

academic standards. Cheering activity became a hybrid of school club and school athletic team, with adult advisor-coaches; competitive qualification to participate; constitutions and written rules of conduct; uniforms; formal budgets; and extensive time commitments to train, practice, perform, and upgrade skills.

Adults' efforts to structure cheerleading began at the collegiate level and influenced secondary school officials who adapted the college activity for younger students. As early as 1924, both Stanford and Purdue universities had established courses in cheerleading to assist students who wanted to try out as yell leaders. Purdue's course, enrolling thirty students in its first year, included tumbling and crowd psychology among topics "to equip the student to rouse and sway masses of people."[2] Stanford offered credit for its course "to sophomores trying out for assistant yell leaders." Topics included "bleacher psychology, the correct use of the voice, development of stage presence, and what a coach expects of the yell leader." The course included lectures by members of the faculty and by football coach Andrew Kerr.[3] Although the *New York Times* reported Stanford's course as straight news, it also editorialized about its value: "How is cheer-leading in the curriculum to be correlated with Life? Football teaches courage, self-restraint and team play. . . . But for what does a course in cheer-leading specifically prepare? For stopping panics in the subway? For nominating Favorite Sons?"[4] In 1924 the value of football is unquestioned, but cheering is yet to be justified on character-building terms.

Public schools followed the colleges, adopting formal tryouts for cheerleaders in lieu of letting students choose among themselves informally. Becoming a school cheerleader meant qualifying and competing for the position, as for an athletic team. In contrast, participating in a pep or rooter club was voluntary and nonexclusive. Schools developed elaborate mechanisms to recruit, train, screen, and elect cheerleaders. Bruce Turvold's 1948 manual suggested that varsity cheerleaders "start a school for future cheerleaders" each year, to instruct hopefuls and practice with them prior to tryouts.[5] The training and selection process used by Washington Park High School of Racine, Wisconsin, in 1950 is indicative of the structured approach used by many schools:

1. On the first day of school an open practice is announced. All interested students are invited to attend.

2. At the first practice all hopefuls do calisthenics, stretching, and running in place. Experienced cheerleaders demonstrate jumps.

3. At the second practice the same exercise routine is done and more difficult jumps are demonstrated.

4. At the third practice the same exercise routine is done and jumps and cheers are practiced individually and in groups.

5. First cut is made. The head coach, female gym teacher, and cheerleading instructor choose ten to twelve girls who will try out at a school assembly.

6. The finalists each choose two cheers to present and another practice is held.

7. At a school assembly the finalists lead one cheer as a group, then each girl leads two cheers by herself. Eight judges (four teachers and four student council officers) rate each girl on crowd appeal, voice, cheering technique, and leadership.

8. Those ranked highest become the "A" squad. The rest become the "B" squad, in training for the next year.[6]

Surely, it was easier to run for student body president than to try out for cheerleading.

Selection of Participants

The first college cheerleaders had been self-selected or chosen by fellow students in recognition of their popularity and influence. By the 1920s, yell leaders were regarded more as official representatives of their colleges and the selection process for collegiate cheerleaders became formalized. At the secondary school level, adult supervisors established criteria and selection processes to promote desired values and behavior in students. The educational importance attached to extracurricular activities is evident in M.L. Staples's 1939 article on the pep assembly as a means to teach students to work together: "The school rally becomes one of the educator's group guidance opportunities for real social service. Booster training is training in the American style of democracy. . . . The school can do no less than provide situations for training in this valuable American trait."[7]

School officials saw cheerleaders as influential student leaders who would demonstrate good behavior and promote it in other students. School supervisors also sought individuals who would perform well as cheerleaders. In 1955 Newark (Delaware) High School listed "desirable traits for cheerleaders," including good manners, responsibility, dependability, leadership ability, scholarship in good standing, and citizenship of high standing, as well as good personal appearance, coordination, and voice.[8] School selection processes emphasized character as well as physical and personality attributes considered appropriate for cheering. Members of the coed Rally Squad at Roosevelt High School in Portland, Oregon, had to qualify on the basis of attendance, grades, behavior (the lack of "any truancies or suspensions"), and health, before the selection committee chose finalists for their "posture, pep personality, and jumping ability." Twelve finalists then tried out before the student body, which elected nine to the squad.[9]

From the publication of *Just Yells*, in 1927, to the present, prescriptive literature on cheerleading has stressed character as well as personality and physical attributes. The 1970 manual, *Cheerleading and Song Leading*, stated that cheerleaders should be "attractive, popular, [and] graceful" in addition to "prompt, dependable . . . able to put duty ahead of personal desires, cooperative . . . good students, and good sports."[10] *The Encyclopedia of Cheerleading* emphasized the cheerleader's influence as an "acknowledged" student leader: "In some cases, the *average* cheerleader has the same power as an *effective* student body president."[11] Selection criteria established by school administrators reinforced this leadership-by-example role. Larry Weber noted in 1981 that "students have to meet disproportionately higher standards to participate in athletics, cheerleading, and student government than . . . [in] journalism, dramatics, clubs, and intramural sports."[12]

By the 1930s and 1940s cheerleader selection processes in schools became structured into rounds of application; practice and training; screening by groups of judges, including teachers, coaches, current cheerleaders, and other student leaders; public tryouts; and election by the student body. This gauntlet allowed for adult control of the applicant pool and for student participation in the final vote, a vestige of the original collegiate process when students chose "the most vibrant and best-liked students . . . because the crowds knew them and were willing to follow them."[13]

In recent years cheerleading tryouts and selection have become increasingly competitive and contentious. Results have been challenged in court by unsuccessful candidates and threats have been made to cheerleading sponsors and other school officials. In some communities, local boosters serve on the judging panels, which may further politicize decisions. In March 1991 the District 348 Board of Education, serving Mt. Carmel, Illinois, voted to change the high school cheerleader selection process, specifying closed sessions with "only the sponsor, candidates, school administration and judges present." Judges were to be members of "a college cheerleading squad from outside Wabash County" and could not be residents of the county. In April 1991 the board was informed that all of the colleges contacted would charge fees and per diem for each judge, and that it would be difficult to arrange a schedule around the college students' classes. The board decided to consider modifications in the process at a later date.[14]

Racial Issues

Issues of race in cheerleading reflect the institutional context of college and school life. As the college experience became available to more women and to middle-class students in the early twentieth century, so did opportunities to participate in extracurricular activities. Participation by black students reflected the segregation of post-secondary institutions. Most black athletes and cheerleaders were limited to segregated colleges and public schools until the Supreme Court's 1954 decision in Brown v. Board of Education of Topeka declared racial segregation to be unconstitutional. The Civil Rights Act of 1964, forbidding racial discrimination in federally funded programs, furthered integration in public schools and colleges. Black athletes were then accepted at predominantly white universities which sought competitive advantage from a wider talent pool.[15]

Without such impetus, acceptance of black cheerleaders at white colleges and universities was a slower process, spurred in some cases by black student activism. In 1967 the Black Student Action Committee at Purdue demanded black representation on the cheerleading squad. Purdue's football team had sixteen black players at the time. A panel of administrators, previous cheerleaders, and others had already selected ten whites, five women and five men, all members of sororities or fraternities, for the 1968 season. As a result of the student committee's pressure, two black women were added to the squad.[16] In 1972 Lou Lillard, a black member of Purdue's squad, was named one of six All-American Cheerleaders at the International Cheerleading Foundation competition held at Madison Square Garden. At an interview during the competition, he said that one reason there were so few black cheerleaders at integrated colleges was the difference in cheering styles at black and white high schools: "The type of cheering at black high schools is . . . more of a stomp-clap, soul-swing thing. . . . At [white] schools, the traditional cheers are straight-arm motions."[17] Most white secondary schools emulated the "traditional" style which had developed in predominantly white colleges.

Black representation on high school cheering squads was also an issue in the late 1960s. In November of 1967, over 1,000 black students boycotted classes for a week at Madison (Illinois) Senior High. They were protesting the suspension of seventeen black football players who had skipped practice to protest that only one of the school's six varsity cheerleaders was black. In response to the boycott, the school board reversed the players' suspensions and agreed that there would be three black cheerleaders on the 1968 squad.[18] In 1969 a youth was killed during two nights of unrest in Burlington, North Carolina, following a school election in which no black cheerleaders were chosen. After a riot at White Plains (New York) High School in 1970, black students demanded that more blacks be placed on the cheerleading squad. In 1971 black representation on the White Plains squad was increased to five of the total fifteen.[19]

In a 1972 *New York Times* interview, cheerleading entrepreneur Lawrence Herkimer commented on the effect desegregation had on black cheerleaders: "[D]esegregation has drastically reduced the number of black cheerleaders, who were often among the very best. The reason . . . is that now there are fewer all-black schools and blacks are not frequently elected in the newly integrated schools where they now constitute a minority."[20] Herkimer also noted that the creation of private, all-white schools in the South had increased his cheerleader uniform-supply business, since each new school fielded its own teams and cheering groups.[21]

The significance of cheerleading in school desegregation was viewed in positive as well as negative terms. Jeffrey Brezner's 1974 study of administrative practices to facilitate integration included "provision for [a] multi-ethnic cheer leading squad."[22] Thomas Collins presented a paper at the American Anthropological Association Meeting in 1977 describing one effect of court-ordered desegregation at a deep-South high school: "[W]hites maintain control over some school activities. [As blacks] have taken over areas such as sports and cheerleading, the status of these [activities] has been refuted by whites."[23]

Concerns about representation were not limited to blacks. In 1969 students in Crystal City, Texas, staged a 28-day walkout to protest the token placement of a single Hispanic cheerleader on the high school squad. The student population at the time was 85 percent Hispanic. Writer Jeannie Ralston lists the walkout as "a seminal event in the birth of the Raza Unida movement."[24]

Cheering continued to be the focus of racial tension at the University of Mississippi. In 1983 the university "disavowed" its long-term association with the Confederate flag as a school symbol, but many students continued to display it. In 1991 Mississippi's faculty senate endorsed a resolution by the alumni association "asking fans to refrain from waving the flag at football games and other events." The request came in response to "student protests in support of a black cheerleader's refusal to carry the flag at football games." The university adopted a new spirit flag and planned to distribute free pom pons at games to discourage continued use of the Confederate flag.[25]

Community Programs

Under adult supervision, cheerleading spread from public secondary schools to elementary schools and to private schools. Catholic schools adopted cheerleading as an activity for girls and supported camps and competitions for secondary school cheerleading squads. Beginning in 1968, the New York Catholic Youth Organizations sponsored an annual cheerleading contest among city schools. The Roman Catholic Diocese of Paterson, New Jersey, ran week-long summer camps for junior and senior high cheering squads.[26]

From the school setting, cheerleading also spread to community-based youth sport programs such as the Pop Warner Football and Young America Football Leagues. Organized youth sports, such as Little League baseball, developed to provide playing experience for boys of elementary school age. As franchises with adult coaches, age-divided leagues, uniforms, and annual tournaments, these community programs became highly structured. Lacking the pedagogical rationale of school sports, community youth sports focused heavily on competitive success. Jonathan Brower, in his study of the psychological impact of such programs, noted that "organized youth sport often becomes an activity in which high-level performance and a 'polished show' is expected. More often than not the players are embroiled in a difficult situation because of adult expectations and demands placed upon them."[27]

Part of the "polished show" included cheerleaders as accessories to the athletic contests. Cheerleading was viewed as an appropriate outlet for girls, who were not permitted to play the sports. For many years the organized youth sports programs were strictly sex-segregated. Boys played football; girls cheered. More recently, girls have been allowed to play Little League baseball, but youth cheering is still defined as a feminine activity. As more sports such as soccer are opened to girls, the division between boys as players and girls as cheerleaders may ease. At present, organized youth sports maintain the same sex-role rigidity as professional sports, while cheering at schools and colleges has been coeducational since the 1920s, and varsity sports for girls have been more widely available since the enactment of Title IX in 1972.[28] Youth sport programs, unlike public school and college sports, are not subject to federal anti-discrimination sanctions. These community-run activities resemble the sexual division in school programs which existed prior to the Title IX era.

Youth sports track children into specific roles at a very early age. Programs such as the Long Island (New York) Midget Football Organization and the New Mexico Young America Football League (YAFL) typically enroll boys and girls aged eight to fourteen. Eight-year-old boys are taught to play football; eight-year-old girls are taught to lead cheers. The division of labor continues in each age grouping. New Mexico's YAFL teams each have twenty-six players and sixteen cheerleaders. In 1991 the YAFL of Albuquerque, New Mexico, had sixty-five teams with 1,600 players and 600 cheerleaders. While the YAFL is a nonprofit organization, annual registration fees are $85.00 per player and $40.00 per cheerleader. Each team has to find a $500 sponsor to help pay for uniforms, equipment, and insurance. Individual player sponsorships allow some low-income children to participate.[29]

Municipal agencies provide some cheerleading activities outside the public school and youth sport programs. The Fayetteville (North Carolina) Parks and Recreation Department and Fairfax (Virginia) County Park Authority have held five-day cheerleading clinics and ten-week classes at $35.00 and $76.00, respectively. Some groups, such as the Washington (D.C.)

Metropolitan Police Boys and Girls Clubs, offer free sports and cheerleading programs to children.[30]

Participation in most community programs is limited to middle-class children whose parents can afford the registration fees and transportation costs. As cheerleading was formalized and incorporated into college, public school, and community programs, participation was determined by adult-developed criteria (including appropriate gender behavior), political factors such as racial segregation, and children's economic status.

Administrative Issues

Governance and discipline of cheering groups have always been a concern of school officials. Many schools adopted written regulations detailing cheerleader conduct. The Pep Club Constitution for Ruskin High School of Hickman Mills, Missouri, specifies cheerleader duties, rules, and penalties for infractions. For instance, those who miss a practice session or chew gum while in uniform may not cheer at the next game; those smoking while in uniform are to be dismissed from the squad; cheerleaders are responsible for decorating the cheering sections of the stands and the goal posts for games.[31]

As school cheering became a structured activity, administrators had to deal with budgeting and funding. A sample cheerleaders' budget for Michigan's Ann Arbor High School in 1946–47 totaled only $54.50, including $30.00 for five uniforms, $14.50 for letter awards and certificates, and $10.00 for megaphones.[32] Expenses increased and proliferated as squads attended training camps, required insurance coverage, and adopted specialized uniforms for indoor as well as outdoor sports. Cheerleader groups have historically done some of their own fund-raising to supplement (or in lieu of) financial support from their schools. Randy Neil's 1975 manual suggested ways for cheerleaders to raise money—renting blankets on cold game days, holding contests where students vote with pennies, washing cars, staging walkathons, and holding auctions and bake sales.[33] In 1989 cheerleaders at Bayard Cobre High School in Bayard, New Mexico, developed a sportsmanship cheer and produced a videotape to promote it throughout the state. They planned to use proceeds from selling the tapes to support their squad.[34]

Budget shortages in the 1980s and 1990s have affected cheerleading along with other extracurricular programs. Some schools have privatized activities as an economy measure. In

Albuquerque, New Mexico, a private company, International Sports Systems, ran the Razzle Dazzle Cheer, Dance, and Drill Teams in eight of the city's twenty-three middle schools. In 1990 over 600 girls participated, at an individual cost of $126 for uniforms plus $25.00 in monthly dues. Some thirty percent of the girls received scholarships from corporate sponsors to enable them to attend. Twenty percent of dues collected were paid to the school system for use of school facilities.[35] In 1991 high schools in Fairfax County, Virginia, curtailed sports seasons, canceled team travel outside the Washington, D.C., area, and restricted freshman and junior varsity cheerleaders to home games in response to budget cuts.[36]

Spirit groups at universities are also affected by cuts in institutional support, unless they receive outside funding from athletic booster clubs. In 1991 the University of New Mexico reallocated $345,000 from student-fee revenues, thereby canceling funding for "cheerleaders, drill team, mascots, collegiate singers and debate team." Funding for the marching band was cut from $150,000 to $75,000.[37]

Legal issues of liability and drug testing are additional concerns which now confront school officials in charge of cheerleading. In 1984 a Minnesota court awarded a high school cheerleader $200,200 for injuries she sustained in a car accident while she and other squad members were delivering banners to the homes of football players prior to a school game. In Vechel vs. Independent School District No. 709, 359 N.W. 2d 579 (Minn. 1984), the court ruled that the adult sponsor appointed by the school did not adequately supervise the cheerleaders in the late-night "bannering," a task they regularly performed as part of their spirit activity.[38]

At the college level, cheerleaders who receive athletic scholarships may face drug testing mandated by the National Collegiate Athletic Association (NCAA). In 1987 the University of New Mexico's cheerleaders, mascots, and dance group were designated as nonscholarship athletes so they would be eligible to receive medical attention from athletic department trainers. Under their new designation as athletes, members of all three groups were tested for drug use. University counsel determined in 1988 that testing was not legally necessary because none of the cheerleaders, mascots, or dancers participated in NCAA competition.[39]

Training for Cheerleaders and Their Advisors

A significant element in the formalization of cheerleading was the impulse to provide in-service training for cheerleaders. The courses offered at Purdue and Stanford in the 1920s were early examples of adult intervention to develop cheering technique and theory. Secondary schools organized short-term clinics as a means to upgrade cheerleading skills, and looked to college cheerleaders for their expertise. According to Brace Turvold, an early proponent of cheer instruction, "[T]he first clinic ever to be held was in Northwood, Iowa, September 21, 1946. This clinic, youth-inspired and youth-planned, aroused a great deal of interest. Since then many schools have started similar clinics in various states."[40] At the Northwood clinic cheerleading squads from area schools gathered for discussions on "pep meetings, outfits, advisors, tryouts, and sportsmanship." Several squads demonstrated cheers, which were critiqued by two women cheerleaders from Iowa's Cornell College. In this initial clinic, high school students sought guidance from collegiate "experts."

The clinic idea caught on with school officials. In 1948 the Magic Valley, Idaho, school district held its first annual cheerleaders' workshop. Topics discussed included "how to be a good loser," "how to be a good winner," "controlling booing," should there always be a boy on the team?, "the rhythm of the yell," "singing with yelling," and "girl cheerleaders must be ladies."[41] These adult-initiated clinics emphasized proper behavior and values over technique.

Evidence of the institutionalization of school cheering is also found in the proliferation of literature defining and describing the role of the adult advisor or sponsor. In 1969 *School Activities* described the functions performed by the cheerleading sponsor at Haltom (Texas) Junior High School. This sponsor, who was also a teacher at the school, reviewed academic records to determine students' eligibility, notified candidates' parents of prospective costs, directed the election campaign, supervised practices for candidates, conducted the election, mailed applications for the summer cheerleading camp the new squad would attend, arranged three practices per week all summer, drove the squad to camp, made sure the squad practiced "almost every day" during fall and spring, helped them arrange pep rallies, took them to all the games (football, once a week; basketball, twice weekly), helped make and put up posters, and arranged a recognition ceremony at the end of the school year.[42] All of this was for seventh- and eighth-graders, but Texas does take cheerleading seriously.

Cheerleader instructor Randy Neil noted: "The devotion that a faculty advisor must have to her job often places her in the position of not only coach, chaperone and sponsor . . . but that of a second parent."[43] Educators continued to stress instructional, guidance, and managerial roles for advisors. In 1978 *Scholastic Coach* published a "Year-round Checklist for the Cheerleading Advisor" and in 1981 the Chicago Board of Education issued *Cheerleading: A Handbook for Teacher-Sponsors.*[44]

Once they established formal cheerleading squads, it did not take long for secondary schools to extend the concept of interscholastic competition to cheering. In at least one instance this was done with an educational rationale. By 1944 the Mid-Hudson Cheerleaders' Association was formed in New York State to promote annual cheerleader meets, competitions among squads from member high schools. The organization's stated purpose for these meets was "to improve the quality of cheerleading . . . through the exchange of ideas and the criticisms . . . of the judges." The association established "criteria for measuring the quality of cheerleading" and sought to "develop and improve" the "fundamental principles and purposes of cheerleading as a science."[45] At the Mid-Hudson meets squads performed before judges who were cheerleading coaches for nonparticipating schools. Competing teams were judged on numerous criteria within the categories of general appearance, technique and skill, synchronization and uniformity, originality and spontaneity, and poise.[46]

Cheerleading competitions run as interscholastic contests by state school activity associations have become increasingly common since the 1970s. In New Mexico the annual state cheerleading and drill team competition is sponsored by the New Mexico Activities Association, which oversees all extracurricular sports, clubs, and performance groups. Competition is divided by size of school and type of spirit group, including cheer with music, precision drill and hand-held props, precision drill and kick, jazz, large group drill, and coed cheerleading.[47]

Educators have instituted an additional form of competition for cheerleaders which promotes desirable academic and behavioral standards. The state of Iowa tracks the grade point averages of cheerleading squads and announces their rankings each year. In 1990, for example, cheerleaders at East Monona

(County) High School, with a combined GPA of 3.61, were rated third statewide.[48] This compares with the practice of publicizing grade point averages of college fraternities and sororities, and the naming of Academic All-Americans in college athletics.

Behavior Control

Adult control of cheerleading activities includes specific control over individual behavior. This degree of adult intervention occurs in various aspects of student life, such as dress codes and attendance requirements, and is common in school athletics, where coaches have authority to dictate a player's weight limit. It is not surprising that adult preferences and school regulations have extended to the control of cheerleaders' physical appearance.

Adolescents put considerable pressure on themselves to conform to peer standards of physical attractiveness. They are influenced by pervasive cultural messages in advertising and entertainment media which stress thinness for females and muscularity for males. These generalized pressures are reinforced by specific demands of authority figures such as coaches and sponsors. Jean Lundholm and John Littrell, in their study of eating disorders among high school cheerleaders, noted: "Various groups of adolescents, such as cheerleaders, dancers, and athletes, often are explicitly and implicitly required to attain and maintain weights that are lower than average for other adolescents of the same height."[49] Lundholm and Littrell surveyed 751 female high-school cheerleaders attending a cheering camp in the Midwest. They found that girls scoring highest on desire for thinness were more likely to engage in bulimic behaviors of binging and purging.[50]

Physical criteria for cheerleaders can be expressed in general terms which imply thinness, such as "fitness," and "overall appearance," but it is not uncommon for specific weight restrictions to be placed on cheerleaders. In 1991 the University of Connecticut withdrew its 125-pound limit for female cheerleaders after Michelle Budnik filed a complaint with the state Commission of Human Rights and Opportunities. Budnik had qualified as a cheerleader at 147 pounds in 1990 but was told she had to meet the 125-pound limit to remain on the squad. She was dropped from the squad when she failed to lose sufficient weight, even though she "resorted to diuretics and laxatives." An official of the university said the policy was originally established "because of concern for the safety of cheerleaders. Since the policy has been changed, male cheerleaders will no longer toss female cheerleaders into the air."[51] Expectations of a more extreme nature can be placed on would-be cheerleaders. In 1986 a California teenager sued the Fountain Valley school district, claiming that a teacher "told her to have breast-reduction surgery if she wanted to join the cheerleading squad."[52]

In the process of formalizing all aspects of cheerleading and making it into a competitive activity, schools restricted cheering to a small minority of students having natural attributes, time, and money sufficient to permit them to participate. Organized youth sports and some municipal programs enabled greater numbers of students to get involved, but money and transportation access were still limiting factors. In at least one school, educators have made the decision to open all activities to any student wanting to participate. The Plainsfield (Indiana) Community Middle School established a "no-cut policy" in 1990. As a result, the school has 72 cheerleaders, a 140-member band, and a 229-member choir. All athletic teams, clubs, and performing groups are open to any student. At a football game with Cascade Junior High, the host school did not want to allow Plainfield's cheerleaders on the field, because cheerleaders are admitted free and Cascade wanted the ticket revenue. The entire squad was admitted "when someone pointed out the amount of sodas and hot dogs they and their parents would buy."[53] This incident represents the best and worst of adult intentions in structured school activities. Pedagogical impulses become warped, reforms are made, and economics continues to play an influential role.

Professionalization of Adult Control

By the 1920s college officials had begun efforts to structure cheerleading, to theorize about it, and to improve its techniques. In the 1940s secondary school educators continued the process, organizing clinics and interscholastic competitions to upgrade skills. Educators were encouraged and assisted in these endeavors by an emerging group of entrepreneurs who published manuals, held instructional clinics and camps, and formed business enterprises to outfit and equip cheerleading squads.

School officials published articles and manuals on cheerleading in the educational literature, but they also relied on a growing body of prescriptive books published commercially by cheerleading enthusiasts. George M. York's *Just Yells: A Guide for Cheer Leaders*, published in 1927, was the first extensive compilation of college and high school yells from throughout the United States. In the same year, Frank A. Gradler published *Psychology and Technique of Cheer-leading: A Handbook for Cheer-leaders.* Gradler focused on advice for the prospective yell leader and described desirable qualities and attitudes.

In 1944 Lawrence M. Brings published *School Yells: Suggestions for Cheerleaders.* Brings solicited schools and colleges to submit their most representative yells, which comprise much of the text. He also included photographs of numerous cheerleading squads. Newt Loken and Otis Dypwick released *Cheerleading & Marching Bands* in 1945. A publisher's note identifies Loken "as one of the greatest of all acrobatic cheerleaders," who introduced "many spectacular and effective acrobatic stunts . . . while he was rooter-king at the University of Minnesota."[54] Their manual included action sequence photographs demonstrating tumbling moves. Bruce A. Turvold issued *The Art of Cheerleading* in 1948, covering all aspects of administering school pep organizations and events as well as cheering techniques.

From the 1950s to the 1980s, dozens of additional titles were published by trade presses and cheer associations. Some, such as *Cheerleading and Baton Twirling* (1970) and *Cheerleading Is For Me* (1981), were aimed at would-be cheerleaders, but most included a combination of cheering techniques and organizational advice useful to sponsors, school administrators, and cheerleaders alike.[55] A current manual for aspiring cheerleaders is Cindy Villarreal's *The Cheerleader's Guide to Life* (1994).

A major force in the professionalization of cheerleading was the formation of companies which offered instructional clinics. At first, in the 1940s, colleges and high schools organized their own workshops, but entrepreneurs were quick to see a demand. Bill Horan, who founded the American Cheerleaders Association in 1949 and Lawrence R. Herkimer, founder of the National Cheerleaders Association (NCA) in 1952, were among the first to offer clinics nationally.[56] Herkimer's clinics were five-day sessions held at college campuses during the summer. By 1956 he was running an annual circuit from June to November, personally conducting clinics on cheering, stunts, pom pon routines, and crowd psychology, In 1956 his National Cheerleaders Association had members in forty-eight states.[57] As business grew, Herkimer added a staff of instructors.

Companies such as the NCA often presented clinics jointly sponsored by local schools and municipalities. The entrepreneurs helped reinforce educators' efforts to structure cheerleading training and competition. In 1967 an NCA instructor presented a one-day clinic to 150 Westchester County (New York) high school cheerleaders who were excused from regular classes in order to attend. The clinic was sponsored by the county for area high schools. Reporting on the clinic, the *New York Times* noted that in ten years with the NCA, instructor Robert Shields had "taught more than 100,000 youths how to cheer more effectively."[58] Other associations followed Herkimer's successful example. Randy Neil established the International Cheerleading Foundation (ICF) in 1964. The ICF had both a university and a scholastic division. In addition to summer clinics, the ICF provided a speakers bureau and uniform-design service and published "spirit textbooks."[59] In 1984 *'Teen* magazine profiled four companies offering cheerleading camps: National Cheerleaders Association, Dallas, Texas; United Spirit Association, Mountain View, California; Universal Cheerleaders Association, Memphis, Tennessee; and Drill Team World, Redondo Beach, California.[60]

Instructional videotapes dealing with cheerleading techniques have become popular in the 1980s and 1990s. Prescriptive literature has contributed outside expertise to cheerleaders, sponsors, and coaches since 1927. Now, training videos promulgate cheerleading standards and styles to an even wider audience. Some, such as *Fundamentals of Cheerleading*, use championship squads from national competitions to demonstrate specific stunts and style.[61]

A body of literature by educators and entrepreneurs has developed since the 1920s to define the principles and practices of cheerleading. A significant, additional influence began in the late 1940s when scholastic cheerleaders organized clinics and invited collegiate cheerleaders as outside experts. Entrepreneurs, including college cheerleaders such as Lawrence Herkimer, were quick to offer clinics and camps on a for-profit basis. These gatherings were an effective means to establish and disseminate cheerleading standards directly to practitioners. Clinics and camps also formed the basis of a thriving industry which equips thousands of school and college cheerleaders annually.

Commercialization—The Business of Cheering

Lawrence R. Herkimer, head of the National Cheerleaders Association, is considered the founding father of the cheer industry. "Herkie" was head cheerleader at Southern Methodist

University in 1947 and 1948. He conducted his first clinic for high school cheerleaders during his last year at SMU. The clinic was arranged by a professor at Sam Houston State "who enlisted an English professor to teach the cheerleaders diction, a physical education instructor to teach them basic gymnastics, and Herkie to teach cheerleading itself."[62]

Herkimer ran the clinic himself the following summer, using cheerleaders as instructors instead of professors. He arranged other week-long clinics at area colleges that were happy to have paying dormitory occupants during summer. The colleges also viewed the visits by high school students as a good recruiting opportunity. By 1951 Herkimer's clinics became a full-time occupation. In addition to summer camps, he offered one-day and weekend sessions throughout the school year.[63] As the NCA grew, Herkimer customized camps and clinics for each type of school. Summer camps were established for cheerleaders from junior colleges, separate from those of larger institutions.[64]

A one-day clinic, organized by Edgewood High School of Ashtabula, Ohio, in 1955, was typical of the symbiotic relationship between cheer professionals and school officials. The Edgewood school planned a Saturday clinic and invited more than 600 area cheerleaders to attend. Lawrence Herkimer was the guest instructor, teaching "effective motions, crowd psychology, sportsmanship, qualifications of a cheerleader, boosting school spirit, and raising funds for cheerleading activities." Other speakers included a principal who spoke on "What the Administrator Expects of a Cheerleading Squad," and Edgewood's head coach, who described "What a Coach Expects of a Cheerleading Squad." Lunch, mass practice sessions, and discussions of individual problems completed the session. All of the 600 girls attending wore their squad uniforms.[65]

Cheer camps became a thriving business. By 1985 the United Spirit Association (USA) had 30,000 students, ages five to eighteen, in 82 camps from Montana to Hawaii. Registration cost $137 for a four-day camp. USA's largest camp, near Santa Barbara, California, had 1,030 girls and 7 boys participating. USA provided separate instruction for cheerleaders, song leaders, drill teams, flag corps, and twirlers.[66] The New York Times reported in 1972 that Lawrence Herkimer grossed $5 million, based on registration fees for some 75,000 camp attendees, and returned $4.5 million to the colleges which served as sites: "The generous split with the colleges discourages his smaller competitors, about six, which operate locally rather than nationally."[67] The number of NCA participants is impressive since only elected cheerleaders were permitted to attend the camps.[68]

The purveyors of camps and clinics diversified to supply cheerleaders with uniforms and equipment and organized competitions to obtain television revenues. At present there are "nearly one million elementary, junior high, high school and college students" leading cheers in America."[69] Equipping them is a lucrative enterprise. It currently costs "a minimum of $200 to outfit a cheerleader with uniforms, pom-poms, shoes, socks, tights and hair ribbons," and while cheering camps are break-even propositions, they are "superb vehicles for the companies' uniforms, which are the real money-makers of the cheerleading business." Nike and Converse shoe companies vie for contracts with the cheerleading suppliers.[70]

In 1991 the two largest firms in the industry were the National Spirit Group, Ltd., the parent company of Lawrence Herkimer's National Cheerleaders Association, and Universal Sports Camps, parent company of Jeff Webb's Universal Cheerleading Association. These companies had combined revenues totaling $75 million in 1991—$45 million to National Spirit Group and $30 million to Universal Sports Camps. The NCA ran 500 camps for 150,000 cheerleaders in 1991, while UCA staged 460 camps for 100,000 attendees.[71]

UCA founder Jeff Webb was an instructor for the NCA prior to starting his own company. Both entities run state, regional, and national cheerleading competitions each year. These contests heighten interest in cheerleading and prompt additional demand for private coaching and choreographic services. Approximately five percent of cheering squads enter these competitions.[72] Webb got ESPN to televise UCA's 1983 high school competition, during which he "ran commercials for his Varsity product line." In 1984 ESPN broadcast UCA's college competition.[73] Cable sports programmers continue to present cheer competitions to their national audience.

Other business people have filled specialized niches in the cheerleading industry. Gwen Sykes-Holtsclaw established Cheer Ltd. in Fayetteville, North Carolina, in 1988. Her specialty is organizing clinics for cheerleading coaches. Over 3,200 coaches attended twelve Cheer Ltd. conferences in 1990. A small company with revenues of $847,000 in 1989, Cheer Ltd. also offers clinics for cheerleaders and has retail and consulting divisions.[74]

With the demand for acrobatics and pyramids in cheerleading, for-profit gymnastics clubs began to market their services to school and college cheerleaders. In 1982 Alexander Douglas, in *International Gymnast* magazine, outlined opportunities at elementary, secondary, and collegiate levels. Douglas noted that many schools lacked space and equipment, such as mats, to enable cheerleaders to practice acrobatics safely. Now local gymnastics clubs routinely advertise cheerleading, tumbling, dance, and stunt training in continuing classes and short-term camps.[75]

Entrepreneurs in the health and fitness industry have begun to target children (or children's parents) with the establishment of "kiddie gyms." These fitness centers provide nutrition programs, games, and sports for children only. One such center, Kidsports of Mesa, Arizona, offers "aerobics, soccer, football, hockey, tumbling, gymnastics, dance, and cheerleading" for separate age groups.[76]

The combined effects of institutionalization and commercialization have made cheerleading an expensive activity. Diana Schumacher, cheerleader sponsor at Churchill High School, San Antonio, Texas, holds a meeting each year with parents to discuss expenses before their children try out. Schumacher estimates the cost at "about $800 for camp, four uniforms with mix-and-match pieces, shoes, megaphone, practice blouses and shorts and other items."[77] This amount does not include gymnastics classes, which many cheerleaders take in order to perform the demanding stunts now common in scholastic and collegiate cheering. Some girls begin taking gymnastics by age seven in preparation for cheerleading. June Blackman-Soffar, owner of Alpha Gymnastics in Houston, Texas, averages 250 to 300 children enrolled for cheerleading each year, at a cost of $70.00 per month. Private lessons cost more.[78]

For some parents the financial burden is too much to bear. In November 1992 a Lexington, Kentucky, man was convicted of writing anonymous, threatening letters to school officials and family members in an attempt to frighten his daughter off her high school cheering squad. Bennie Lee Doan admitted that he wrote the letters because "he could not afford the expenses" for his daughter to remain on the squad.[79]

The institutionalization of cheerleading involves adult control in a variety of contexts. As an educational device, it is supervised by school personnel; as a community youth program, it is overseen by parent-volunteers; and as a profitable business, it is promoted by entrepreneurs. These adult agendas have shaped cheering into a complex and demanding endeavor which operates at many levels beyond the recreational diversion students originally created for themselves.

3

From Those Who Yell to Those Who Sell: Cheerleading in Professional Sports

There are certain parallels between collegiate and professional cheerleading. Both originated to support football and both added entertainment and pageantry to the evolving phenomenon of spectator sport. What has come to be known as professional cheerleading, however, owes more to the drill team and dance team than to the cheerleading squad. While school and college cheering eventually fostered a supporting industry of suppliers and instructors, professional cheerleading was designed from its beginnings as a subsidiary of the professional sports industry.

The development of professional cheerleading was shaped by the mass entertainment and promotional demands of professional sport. These demands created a paradox for team management—how to exploit a consciously sexual sell while avoiding the appearance of sexual impropriety. The resulting tension between "good" and "bad" publicity continues to be reflected in the image of the professional cheerleader.

History

In the 1920s the collegiate emphasis on spirit activities such as fight songs, yell leaders, and marching bands influenced professional as well as scholastic sport. The Chicago Bears and the Frankford (Pennsylvania) Yellow Jackets had their own fight songs in the 1920s, well before the Washington Redskins adopted their now-famous "Hail to the Redskins" in 1937.[1] In 1924 *The Literary Digest* reported on efforts to organize cheering sections at professional baseball games. The baseball cheerleaders did not emulate the "clean-cut, loyal, sportsmanlike" college yell leaders of the era: "Instead of rooting for their home team . . . [the baseball cheerleaders] concentrated in attacks on the visiting team."[2] To date, although cheerleading has expanded to professional sports such as basketball and soccer, it is still not associated with professional baseball.

George Marshall, owner of both the Washington Redskins and a radio broadcasting network, was an early proponent of collegiate-style hoopla to promote his football team. In 1936 he was the first to employ a marching band to play at elaborately choreographed halftime spectacles for a professional football team. In 1937 he followed the collegiate model when he sent his 150-member band by train to New York City to support the Redskins in the Eastern Division title game.[3] Marshall was the first pro football owner to broadcast games nationwide on radio. This exposure, along with the musical spectacles, helped make the Redskins nationally popular by the 1940s.[4] Marshall's approach pioneered promotional and marketing devices now commonplace in professional sports management.

During the 1950s and 1960s some professional football teams used cheerleading groups, usually high school students who worked as volunteers. The Baltimore Colts had cheerleaders beginning in 1954.[5] In the early 1960s the Washington Redskins featured a group of young women dressed as Indian princesses who marched with the band and performed pom pon routines during games.[6] The formation of the American Football League (AFL) and the expansion of the National Football League (NFL) in 1960 created new teams, such as the Denver Broncos and the Dallas Cowboys, which needed to develop fan support immediately.[7] In 1960 the Cowboys' new general manager, Tex Schramm, hired high school teacher Dee Brock to organize a group of cheerleaders. Schramm's idea was to use attractive models as cheerleaders, but Brock argued that models who knew nothing about cheering "would never sustain fan interest." She lobbied instead for a coed group of thirty high school students. This squad of collegiate-style cheerleaders, named the "Belles and Beaux," served from the first Cowboys game in 1961 through 1971.[8] *The Official 1982 Dallas Cowboys Bluebook* notes that the Belles and Beaux "were virtually unnoticed as they tried to persuade disinterested Cotton Bowl crowds to do the traditional 'two bits, four bits' sort of cheers."[9] At Schramm's insistence a jazz dance team was formed in 1972, and the success of the Dallas Cowboys Cheerleaders would prove his original inclination prophetic indeed.

Dance and drill teams, another form of school and college pageantry, were also used to add color to professional football games by the 1960s. Early prototypes were small groups of female dancers such as the UCLA Song Girls and drill teams, groups of

40 to 100 dancers who marched and danced to band music. Drill teams provided the model for such groups as the Dolphin Dolls, "a precision dance team of conservatively dressed teen-age girls," who performed for the Miami Dolphins from 1966 through 1978."[10]

Credit for inventing the drill team goes to Gussie Nell Davis, who organized the Kilgore College Rangerettes of Kilgore, Texas, in 1940. Davis, a teacher who had trained high school marching drill groups, was hired in 1939 by the Kilgore College president, a Baptist who wanted to encourage alcoholic temperance during football games. He ordered Davis "to produce a halftime show that would keep the men in their seats instead of under the stands taking a nip." Her first show in 1940 included fireworks and a "drill-and-dance group" which inspired "unaccustomed sobriety."[11] The short-skirted, high-kicking Rangerettes of Kilgore Junior College were an immediate success, inspiring imitators throughout Texas high schools and colleges. They have appeared at numerous national events, including all Cotton Bowl games from 1951 to the present, Macy's Thanksgiving Day parades, and Dwight Eisenhower's first inaugural.[12]

As professional football teams began to establish themselves in the new medium of television, they could not fail to notice the broadcast exposure which drill groups such as the Rangerettes and the Tyler Junior College Apache Belles received in the 1950s. Fledgling football franchises such as the Dallas Texans used drill teams at their games to provide halftime entertainment. The Tex Anns performed for the franchise in the 1960s until the team was transferred and reconstituted as the Kansas City Chiefs."[13]

By 1973, twenty-one of the twenty-six clubs in the National Football League employed groups of young women for promotional and public relations appearances.[14] Groups such as the San Francisco 49ers Nuggets were another prototype for the professional cheerleading squad. Established in 1970, the Nuggets served as "white-booted ambassadors" who made public appearances to "sell the San Francisco 49ers." They would typically appear at a department store or golf tournament, pass out team decals and bumper stickers, and sign autographs. At first, the young women who served as Nuggets did not perform: "Their primary duty was to look sexy, and at that they were a complete success."[15] In 1974 the Nuggets added entertainment to their promotion duties. Dressed in red hot-pants, red tops over white, long-sleeved shirts, white cowboy hats, and white, knee-high boots, they did dance routines and sang songs as part of pregame and halftime shows.[16]

From the 1950s to the early 1970s, the presence of high school cheerleaders, drill teams, and promotional groups in professional football helped set the stage for a phenomenon which captivated the National Football League in 1976. In 1972 the formation of a dance group in the Dallas Cowboys organization set a standard to be imitated by nearly every NFL team. The Dallas Cowboys Cheerleaders soon came to symbolize the essence of professional cheerleading: glamour, sex appeal, celebrity, and merchandising success.

Cowboys general manager Tex Schramm, who was persuaded to use high school cheerleaders instead of models in 1960, requested a change when the Cowboys moved to their new stadium in 1971. He wanted beautiful girls who could dance like the Kilgore Rangerettes.[17] Schramm was quoted in *Playboy* in 1978: "We reevaluated our fans' response to the kind of cheerleaders we'd had . . . from the outset . . . we changed our approach . . . and decided to make our cheerleaders more or less atmosphere producers."[18]

Texie Waterman, a Dallas native and successful Broadway choreographer, was hired "to bring New York-style jazz dancing to the fifty-yard line."[19] Waterman was charged with conducting tryouts, selecting dancers, and choreographing routines.[20] To add to the "atmosphere," Paula Van Waggoner was commissioned to design new uniforms. Her midriff-baring hot-pants ensembles, considered risque in 1972, proved to be so popular they remained virtually unchanged for twenty years.[21] The new-look squad of seven dancers debuted in Texas Stadium in 1972, generating some controversy and immediate local popularity. It would be several years before the Dallas Cowboys Cheerleaders became a national sensation. In retrospect, their founding is acknowledged as the beginning of professional cheerleading.

Dallas's national influence began during Super Bowl X, when the Cowboys played the Pittsburgh Steelers.[22] As team publicity reported: "It all began in the blink of an eye back in January 1976 when a Dallas Cowboys cheerleader, standing on the sidelines in Miami's Orange Bowl, winked at the attending network television cameras."[23] Dallas lost the game, but the cheerleaders won a national audience. Television broadcasters and viewers alike recognized "the beginning of a phenomenon" and the Dallas squad became "new darlings of the sports world."[24] By spring

1976, demand for appearances by the Dallas cheerleaders increased so much that Schramm hired Suzanne Mitchell to direct their public relations activity.[25]

The demand for "go-go dancers on the sidelines" swept the National Football League.[26] Other teams rushed to establish dance groups or replace their high school cheerleaders with "slightly older, sexier and scantily-dressed women."[27] The Miami Dolphins replaced their teenaged drill team with the Miami Starbrites dancers and hired nationally known June Taylor as choreographer.[28] By 1978 the Chicago Honey Bears, Denver's Pony Express, and the Baltimore Colts cheerleaders were organized.[29] Other groups included the San Diego Chargerettes, New Orleans Angels, Cincinnati Ben-Gals, the Buffalo Jills, the Los Angeles Rams Embraceable Ewes, Houston's Derrick Dolls, the Philadelphia Liberty Belles, Kansas City Chiefettes, Oakland Raiderettes, and the Washington Redskinettes.[30]

The development of professional football was fostered by the growing popularity of television from the 1950s onward. The new medium broadcast games regionally and nationally, reaching audiences far beyond a team's home city. Changes in production technology enhanced a viewer's ability to follow the action of the game. In 1964 the CBS network first used an "isolated camera" in addition to the six or seven cameras usually employed to televise an NFL game. The isolated camera focused close-up on selected players during each play and provided detailed shots for "post-play reruns," now institutionalized as the "instant replay."[31] The isolated close-up was also used for human interest shots of individuals in the stands and players on the bench. With the introduction of sexy dance troupes on the sidelines, television directors had a ready source of appealing visuals during the numerous breaks in game action. The famous wink which captivated a Super Bowl audience in 1976 was typical of local camera shots familiar to Dallas viewers since 1972.

The "honey shot" became a staple of television sports broadcasting, with ABC television sports director Andy Sidaris one of its most avid proponents. Sidaris, characterized by *Los Angeles* magazine as "the man who brings T & A [tits and ass] from the gridiron to your home" and "is to cheerleaders what Hugh Hefner has been to centerfolds," cheerfully stated his view: "Once you've seen one huddle you've seen them all. . . . So you either look at the popcorn, the guys, or the ladies. The choice is clear for me."[32] Despite ABC's stated intention to deemphasize cheerleader shots in 1979, it was noted that when Sidaris directed a *Monday Night Football* game between the Dallas Cowboys and Los Angeles Rams, "the Cowboys were practically invisible; [while] the Dallas Cowboys Cheerleaders . . . were seen everywhere but on the blimp."[33] The new cheerleader dance groups were styled to appeal to television and television readily complied.

The sudden proliferation of professional cheerleaders raised some controversy. Columnist Ann Landers ran a letter from an angry reader who complained about "older, sexier, and more naked cheerleaders" in the NFL.[34] In 1978 *Jet* magazine juxtaposed two controversies, women cheerleaders "shaking their short-shorts" on the field and women sports reporters doing interviews in the locker room. *Jet* editorialized cautiously about women's role in both situations.[35] Oakland Raiders coach John Madden wondered if cheerleading and football would reverse roles:

> I can see what this game is coming to. Choreographers instead of coaches. It will be a contest to judge which set of girls gets more TV time . . . the losing choreographer will tell the press, "We lost our momentum. . . . We'll have to regroup, go back to fundamentals." . . . And after the girls have competed, the football players will come out at halftime for their exhibition, but the press won't notice because they'll be too busy watching replays of the cheerleaders.[36]

Local controversy developed when some NFL cheerleaders posed for *Playboy*. In 1979 two members of Denver's Pony Express were dismissed for appearing in a *Playboy* feature on cheerleaders. Pony Express members were required to sign contracts which prohibited being photographed for any publication or using the Pony Express name without permission. One of the women argued that she had not technically violated any agreement since as choreographer she had not signed the regular contract, but she was dismissed as well.[37] Reactions varied among NFL organizations. Some clubs did not object; others, like the Baltimore Colts and Denver, fired cheerleaders who posed.[38] In the spring of 1980 the Denver Broncos announced that the Pony Express was disbanded and that area high school students would be asked to serve as cheerleaders instead. "Increasing costs and image problems" were cited as contributing factors for the decision.[39]

Local conflicts notwithstanding, by 1981 seventeen of the NFL clubs had cheerleading squads totaling 580 members. The only teams not fielding cheerleading groups were Cleveland, Denver, Detroit, Minnesota, New Orleans, New York, Pittsburgh, San Diego, and San Francisco.[40]

The cheerleading phenomenon spread to professional basketball and soccer as well. *Newsweek* reported in 1977 that the Washington Bullets had just introduced the Bullettes, "who do the hustle at time outs," and that the Los Angeles Lakers and the Atlanta Hawks were also forming troupes.[41] By 1981 the Laker Girls were a regular feature at Los Angeles Lakers basketball games. Pop singer Paula Abdul, one of twelve Laker Girls in 1981, became the group's choreographer before launching her singing career.[42] The Laker Girls are one group which approaches the Dallas Cowboys Cheerleaders in media recognition. Both troupes have the popular distinction of being featured in a made-for-TV movie.

The trend for cheerleaders in professional basketball continues. In 1990 the Denver Nuggets announced formation of a dance team and a video to promote recently hired coach Paul Westhead's new offensive and defensive system.[43] Professional soccer was quick to imitate the trend set by football. In 1979 *Soccer* magazine featured articles on "The Great NASL Cheerleader Explosion" and "The Making of a Cosmos Girl."[44] By 1983 cheerleading had also come to professional indoor soccer.[45]

The prominence of cheerleading in the promotion of professional football is evident in the expansion of football in Canada in the late 1970s, to England and Europe in the 1980s, and to new markets in the United States in the 1980s and 1990s. *Maclean's* magazine reported that a promotional tour by the Dallas Cowboys Cheerleaders caused "a near riot" when they appeared at the Toronto Sportsman's Show in March 1978. By 1978 Canadian Football League clubs had cheerleading groups in the Dallas mode including the Edmonton Q-Tees, the Ottawa Silver Machine, the Argo Sunshine Girls, Montreal's Les Gentilles Alouettes, the Calgary Outriders, and the Saskatchewan Golden Girls.[46] The establishment of the United States Football League (USFL) saw new clubs such as the Oakland Invaders holding dance auditions for cheerleading squads in 1983.[47]

In 1986 the NFL began to promote American-style football in England with events such as the annual American Bowl, a preseason game between NFL teams played in London. The

Albuquerque Journal noted in 1987 that American football "is a rapidly growing sport in England, with telecasts of National Football League games getting high ratings and more than 90 teams playing in a nationwide semipro league. The cheerleaders, bands and other sideshows of pro football have been part of its appeal in Britain."[48] The *Journal* compared the arrivals of the Denver Broncos and the Los Angeles Rams, scheduled to play in the second American Bowl, in 1987. While the Broncos "flew quietly into Gatwick Airport . . . the Rams arrived at Heathrow Airport complete with all the hoopla"—Rams cheerleaders greeting the plane, a band playing, and team representatives handing out T-shirts to the crowd.[49]

The British journal *Leisure Management* reported that there were 198 men's teams with 16,000 players participating in American-style football in England by 1988. Citing the emphasis on entertaining spectators with "pre-game shows, marching bands, [and] cheerleaders," the article included a dressing room for cheerleaders in its checklist of facilities needed to stage a game.[50]

The World League of American Football (WLAF) was formed in 1991 to bring spring football to United States and European markets. Characterized as "a made-for-television league," the WLAF adopted rules to speed up the game, encouraged player celebrations after touchdowns, and featured a "helmet-cam," miniaturized technology to record action from the player's point of view.[51] WLAF teams also featured the tried-and-true device of cheerleader dance groups. In 1992 *Entertainment Tonight* reported on American-style cheerleading for Europe's WLAF teams. The Barcelona Dragon Girls were said to be "celebrities in their own right"; the London Monarch Crown Jewels performed in a soccer stadium behind a wire barrier between the field and the stands; and the Frankfurt Galaxy squad, which had an American choreographer, cheered in English and German.[52]

In 1992 the Professional Spring Football League (PSFL), was established to field football teams in cities lacking NFL franchises. Although the league was working on a small scale financially, it planned to have cheerleader dance groups for its teams. The proposed PSFL Albuquerque Rattlesnakes, not yet organized as a team, held dance tryouts for a cheerleading troupe.[53] Cheerleading has become a staple element in professional football, basketball, and, to a lesser extent, soccer.

Participants

Professional cheerleaders are selected according to criteria which were effectively established with the debut of the Dallas Cowboys Cheerleaders in 1972. Visual sex appeal and the ability to dance were the primary qualifications and they continue to be so twenty years later. Since a male audience is the primary market group for professional team sports, attractive, youthful, female cheerleaders are chosen to appeal to that audience.

In terms of gender, professional cheerleading is more restrictive than collegiate and scholastic cheering, where both male and female participants are permitted. Since the stylistic content of professional cheerleading is dance rather than yells and acrobatics, the more appropriate parallel is the dance-drill team popularized by high schools and colleges. These groups were always female, when contemporary cheerleading squads were male, female, or coeducational. Dance appears to be the salient variable. Beginning in the 1940s, the dance-drill team's use of chorus-line high-kicks and other dance moves defined it as a feminine activity. Professional cheerleading, in following the drill-team model, was also defined as feminine.

Racially, most professional cheerleading groups have been diverse. Dallas has employed black cheerleaders since 1972.[54] Five of the thirty-two members of the 1979 Denver Pony Express were black.[55] The 1981 Dallas Cowboys Cheerleaders squad of thirty-six had one Asian and four black members.[56] In 1981 *Ebony* magazine reported that every NFL cheerleading squad except the Green Bay Packers had black members, and that the Philadelphia Eagles had the largest number, with ten black cheerleaders.[57] Given the prominence of black players in professional football and basketball and the racial diversity of the sports audience, it made marketing sense to include black, Hispanic, and Asian women on the cheerleading squads.

In terms of socioeconomic status, professional cheerleaders come from a variety of backgrounds. They range in age from eighteen to the early thirties. They are single, married, and single parents. Their occupations range from college student, secretary, physical therapist, actress, computer programmer, model, receptionist, clerk, bank manager, dance instructor, housewife, hairdresser, waitress, dental hygienist, and medical technician to former Marine.[58] In 1986 Sylvia Rose, a Washington Redskinette, was featured in *Sporting News* as a notable anomaly: a professional cheerleader working on her law degree at Georgetown University, and married to Donovan Rose, a defensive back for the rival Miami Dolphins.[59]

Some professional cheerleaders have been school or college cheerleaders, but many have not. The experience of performing before school crowds is transferable to professional cheerleading, even if tumbling skills and yelling are not. What most professional cheerleaders have in common is formal dance training or experience. As 1981 Dallas Cowboys Cheerleader Anita Jefferson observed: "I don't believe that a person without a dance background could join the Cheerleaders and perform at our level. That used to be the case, but not now."[60]

Motivations to become a professional cheerleader are varied. Some women have career aspirations in acting, modeling, or dance and hope the experience (and exposure) as a cheerleader will help them in other aspects of show business. The career ladder in professional cheerleading is limited. One can become a director of a professional cheerleading group, but there are only about twenty such positions in the NFL. Susie Walker, a 1990 cheerleader for the Kansas City Chiefs, is an unusual example of career progression. After cheering at Kutztown High School in Kutztown, Pennsylvania, Walker was a cheerleader at the University of Delaware. During summers, she taught at cheerleading camps which led to a full time job with the International Cheerleading Foundation in 1989. The Foundation directs cheering camps and also runs the Chiefs' cheerleading program. Walker, as an ICF staff member, is assistant director of the squad and a Chiefs cheerleader.[61] This situation is unique since most professional sports teams manage their cheerleading groups themselves and few active cheerleaders are also managers.

Pop singer Paula Abdul is one person who parlayed cheering into an entertainment career. Abdul, who took "hours and hours" of dance lessons as a child, became a Laker Girl in 1981 and soon took over as choreographer for the group. Fans liked the "jazzy dance steps and savvy street moves" she added to routines. She received offers to choreograph commercials and music videos for Janet Jackson, ZZ Top, and the Pointer Sisters. She also choreographed the films *Coming to America* and *The Running Man*. Her music video work led to her own Emmy-winning recording and dancing career.[62] Abdul says, "I owe a lot to being a Laker Girl."[63]

Other motivations to become a cheerleader for a professional team include being a fan, the opportunity for an active social life, a strong sense of group affiliation, a chance at celebrity, and a sense of accomplishment in competing and performing. Financial rewards are minor. Salaries of $15.00 "before taxes" per game were common in the 1970s and 1980s for what amounts to a halftime job when rehearsals and performances are included. Additional reimbursements for promotional appearances depend on team policy. In 1990 salaries of $50.00 per game were the norm, still below minimum wage when all preparation time is included.[64]

For some women, socialized from childhood to compete in beauty pageants, the auditions and tryouts are a competitive outlet. As former Dallas cheerleader Suzette Scholz put it: "The dream of every little girl . . . in the whole state of Texas . . . is to join the Dallas Cowboys Cheerleaders—or become Miss America, which [is] about the same thing."[65]

Some are attracted to the social opportunities available to a professional cheerleader. Oakland Raiderette Gale Carter put it directly: "I have access to parties, players, the big time. They call it life in the fast lane."[66] Personal friendships and close-knit group identity are another motivation for some cheerleaders. Ingrid Soehn, member of the disbanded Pony Express, said, "I don't think people realized how close we were, especially those who were there all three years [of the squad's existence]."[67] Jody Jones, another ex-Pony Express member, later tried out as cheerleader for the Denver Avalanche, an indoor soccer team, because "It's a chance to regain those friendships, to be part of a group, to be dedicated to something."[68] Although they have few opportunities to play on professional sports teams, some women can approximate aspects of that experience via the surrogate cheering squad.

The opportunity for local and even national celebrity is a strong motivating factor for cheerleaders. Dallas cheerleader Suzette Scholz anticipated the impact of that experience: "I wasn't trying out for some cheerleading squad. I was auditioning to be a celebrity who would be whisked off into a fairy tale for a year. I was going to be a movie star, a beauty queen, and a member of an internationally known dance troupe that toured the world."[69] Dallas cheerleaders have appeared in television movies and specials, which is not the norm for most squads, but all pro cheerleaders become local celebrities by definition. As Washington Redskinette Syndi Stewart said, "We're like movie stars without movies."[70] National celebrity (and notoriety) is a prospect any cheerleader may encounter. Professional cheerleaders, like all entertainers, are fair game for the national tabloid press. A 1992 *National Enquirer* story on television personality Alan Thicke's relationship with L.A. Raiders cheerleader, Alethia Williams, is typical.[71]

Many cheerleaders cite a sense of accomplishment and exhilaration competing for the job and performing during games. Dallas cheerleader Suzette Scholz stated: "If you're from Texas and one day you get chosen to be a Cowboys Cheerleader, it's right up there with your wedding day. And depending on who you marry, it might even be bigger."[72] Oakland Raiderette Gwen Thompson also made comparisons with a major life event: "When they call your number and you know you've made the squad, it's an unbelievable feeling. The only thing that's ever topped it was giving birth to my son."[73] When asked why she pursued cheerleading, Philadelphia Liberty Belle Sandee Nehring responded: "You're part of something larger than life. One hundred million people saw us cheer at the Super Bowl—and that makes you feel part of something spectacular."[74]

Entertainment and Promotional Functions

The original function of college and school cheerleading was to rally crowd support to inspire team performance during an athletic contest. The main functions of professional cheerleading are to entertain the crowd during breaks in the game and, quite apart from games, to promote the corporate interests of the team through public appearances, advertising, and merchandising. Instead of leading crowd yells, professional cheerleaders do dance routines. They perform on the sidelines, a vestige of collegiate cheering, but they are present as entertainers, not as motivators. Although they do not lead cheers, they are almost always referred to as cheerleaders. It would be more accurate to call them chorus girls or show girls, but the cheerleader label is another vestige of the collegiate tradition.

The show business and promotional aspects of professional cheerleading are reflected in the emphasis on dance skill, personality, and sex appeal as selection criteria. Choreographer Texie Waterman is credited with creating "sports entertainment dancing," for the Dallas Cowboys Cheerleaders. She developed a style of jazz dance "that exploded onto the field . . . big steps, big movements, big kicks."[75] To present dance successfully in a giant football stadium, the cheerleaders had to be good dancers. Pat

McDonald, director of Philadelphia's Liberty Belles, described her criteria for a cheerleader: "Good looks are important, but she must have talent—be . . . a fine dancer, and have a sense of movement and music. You'd be amazed at how beautiful our rejects are."[76]

Ron Chapman, a Dallas radio personality who judged auditions for Cowboys cheerleaders, observed that if a candidate had the desired quality—whether it be "verve," "charisma," or "sparkle"—"it would come out only on the dance floor."[77] Attractive physical appearance is another major criterion. When the New Jersey Generals held dance auditions for cheerleaders they also assessed "face, hair, walk, posture, smile, grooming, overall body, confidence, expression, and projection."[78]

Each professional franchise conducts its own cheerleader selection process. Most involve some combination of open tryouts, dance auditions, and personal interviews. There are parallels with the beauty pageant: a variety of judges from the community, talent competition, and elimination of candidates in successive rounds. The Dallas Cowboys use an elaborate two-month process to evaluate thousands of applicants yearly. Two thousand hopefuls dance individually in the preliminary round; 150 advance to semifinals where they are taught a new dance routine. Their ability to learn quickly is an important factor in advancing to the final round. Finalists have a week "to prepare for an exam on football, write an autobiography and develop a talent presentation. Personal interviews are conducted with all finalists."[79] Veteran members automatically advance to the finals, but must compete annually against all new finalists for a spot on the squad.

In 1983 the Oakland Invaders used audience participation to select their Blue Angels troupe. After a series of open tryouts at area shopping malls, the team's choreographer selected sixty-two finalists to perform at the Oakland Coliseum. After brief interviews, each contestant did a dance routine while close-up and full-length photos of her were projected on a large screen in the arena. Based on an audience applause meter, thirty women were then selected to the team.[80]

If the ordeal of tryouts appears to be excessive, the physical demands of rehearsing and performing are considerable as well. Professional cheerleaders are "on-stage" for at least five to six hours on game days. They perform before kickoff, on the sidelines throughout the game, and may remain an hour after the game, signing autographs. For an hour prior to performing they warm up, stretch, and run through routines. Dallas Cowboys Cheerleaders perform an eight-minute pregame dance, do different sets after each quarter of play, and dance to every song played by the band during each time-out of the three-hour game.[81]

To prepare for game conditions, where the temperature on the field of Texas Stadium can reach 130 degrees, Dallas cheerleaders rehearse indoors in summer without air conditioning. They rehearse up to four hours a night, three to five nights per week to build stamina for the season.[82] Cheerleaders in northern climates endure below-zero wind-chill conditions during games.

Dance groups learn between thirty-five and fifty routines each season.[83] Suzanne Mitchell, director of the Dallas Cowboys Cheerleaders, estimated that each five-minute dance represents thirty hours of practice.[84] In addition to rehearsals, cheerleaders must do daily stretching exercises to maintain flexibility for high-kicks.[85] Dance is the primary element of mass entertainment provided by professional cheerleaders, but a considerable portion of their job involves personal appearances and public relations in venues far removed from stadium sidelines.

Professional cheerleading groups were originally created to add to the entertainment surrounding football games. The cheerleaders proved to be so popular and "media-genic" that team management seized on their potential for publicity and marketing. Professional teams eagerly sought the favorable publicity generated by their cheerleader groups, and took measures to prevent negative publicity which sometimes occurred as well.

As popular local personalities, cheerleaders are in demand for public appearances in the community. In Dallas's case the group developed a national following and made international appearances in addition to visiting local hospitals, rest homes, orphanages, and charity events.[86] The Denver Broncos' Pony Express made appearances at a United Way luncheon, Children's Hospital Christmas party, city parades, and charity events for the March of Dimes, American Cancer Society, and Muscular Distrophy Foundation.[87] Miami Dolphin Cheerleaders modeled "Love Me, Read to Me" T-shirts at the Broward County (Florida) Library in 1988 to promote its Year of the Young Reader campaign.[88] Public relations work of this nature quickly became a part of the professional cheerleader's job.

The cheerleader troupes developed their own fan following. Suzette Scholz recalled how the Dallas Cowboys Cheerleaders would spend an hour after games signing autographs for "thousands" of waiting fans: "The Cowboys players and Cheerleaders dressed and exited on opposite sides of the stadium, so the people who lined up outside our [exit] were exclusively Dallas Cowboys Cheerleaders fans."[89]

Some groups were in such demand they did not need media attention to promote themselves further. Mardy Medders, director of the Los Angeles Rams Cheerleaders, said, regarding press coverage, "Who needs the ink? I have 400 shows scheduled for the coming year—television, USO tours, county fairs, charities, [and] fashion shows."[90] Suzanne Mitchell attested to the intense demand for the Dallas Cheerleaders: "I have never gone to anyone and asked if we could appear anywhere and we have never sought out anyone to do our merchandising. They have always come to us. I have never solicited one piece of business . . . [and] I turn down 90 per cent of the requests that come in."[91]

Exclusivity is a successful marketing device. In the 1990s Mitchell's successor, Leslie Haynes, continues to reject most of the hundreds of proposals Dallas receives for "marketing ideas and commercial endorsements." This has prevented "consumer burnout" and probably heightened interest in the Dallas cheerleaders, whose involvement in merchandising has been extensive.[92] Items such as "posters, playing cards, calendars, dolls, frisbees, jewelry, T-shirts, decals, bubble gum, trading cards, boots, caps, jigsaw puzzles, [and] kids' clothing," featuring the Dallas cheerleaders, or autographed by them, have been "merchandised all over the world."[93]

In addition to public appearances, cheerleaders are used to promote the parent team in a variety of ways. In 1978 the Minnesota Vikings produced a poster featuring their Parkettes Cheerleaders. The St. Louis Park High School students who served as Vikings cheerleaders normally wore sweaters and skirts, but the poster featured women in leotard costumes with fishnet hose and white boots. Two of the five women pictured were former Parkettes, including one blonde chosen because there were "too many brunettes." In order to sell the Vikings, management substituted a sexier, more provocative image for the wholesome appearance of the actual cheerleading squad.[94]

The *Official 1982 Dallas Cowboys Bluebook*, promoting all aspects of the team, featured small black-and-white photographs of the players, but full-color portraits of the cheerleaders in their costumes. Dallas management consciously emphasized the allure of the cheerleaders over that of the players.[95]

During the 1987 NFL season the Minnesota Vikings capitalized on controversy generated when Chicago Bears coach Mike Ditka referred to the Minneapolis Metrodome stadium as the "Rollerdome." In response, Vikings general manager Mike Lynn sent Ditka a pair of Rollerblades and the Vikings' cheerleaders did a routine wearing Rollerblades at the next Minnesota-Chicago game.[96] The Vikings used their cheerleading squad in a clever gimmick to gain positive publicity in the wake of Ditka's remark.

From management's point of view, the down side of cheerleading groups' popularity and celebrity is the potential for scandal and negative publicity. Most pro teams regulate cheerleaders' behavior and react strongly when individuals flout regulations and embarrass the parent organization. The tension between "good" and "bad" publicity has continued to exist since the 1970s. "Good" publicity is any media exposure authorized by team management. "Bad" publicity is any unauthorized exposure of a cheerleader's sexuality. It is "good" if cheerleaders generate media attention as a sexy (but wholesome) group. It is "bad" if they garner attention as sexy individuals.

There were no immediate repercussions when a member of Denver's Pony Express was arrested in 1978 "in connection with the theft of a wallet from an undercover policeman posing as a drunk."[97] However, when several Pony Express members posed for a *Playboy* pictorial in 1978, it "sparked a furor" of controversy in Denver. When two other Pony Express cheerleaders posed for *Playboy* in 1979, they were dismissed from the squad, and in March 1980 the Broncos disbanded the Pony Express altogether. Broncos publicity director Jim Saccomano cited "negative publicity" as a factor in the decision, but confirmed that the Broncos "weren't dissatisfied with the public response to the Pony Express during its three years."[98] Publicity of the desired sort was fine, but controversial publicity was sufficient reason to jettison the troupe.

Reaction to the *Playboy* pictorials varied among NFL teams. *Women's Sports* reported, "Some encouraged the cheerleaders to pose . . . and some told the women that if they [posed] they would lose their jobs."[99] The San Diego Chargers fired cheerleader Lynita Shilling, who posed, and fired all other squad members, even though they did not pose.[100] Jackie Rohr, a Chicago Honey Bear who was fired, noted the inconsistency in team officials' attitudes: "When they took our pictures for a poster shot, the Bears office told us to wear pushup bras, show lots of cleavage, really schmaltz it up. When they heard I'd posed nude, they called *that* distasteful."[101] The sexual sell is permissible when sanctioned by team management, but individual free-lancing is discouraged.

A more recent example of good/bad (or bad/good) publicity is the publication of *Deep in the Heart of Texas*, an account by sisters Suzette, Stephanie, and Sheri Scholz of their experiences as Dallas Cowboys Cheerleaders in the 1980s. In addition to their own stories, the Scholz sisters interviewed 150 other former Dallas cheerleaders and acknowledge using composites of people and events "for dramatic purposes."[102] While the Scholz book describes the glamour and excitement of the Dallas phenomenon, it also details criminal drug abuse, substance abuse to meet draconian weight restrictions, and manager Suzanne Mitchell's demeaning emotional manipulation of the cheerleaders. As both paean and exposé, the message is mixed. The Cowboys organization, which did not authorize publication, no doubt winced at some of the book's revelations, yet benefited from the national publicity it generated.

Professionalization and Control

Professional cheerleading incorporates aspects of mass entertainment and big business, both of which are central to professional sport. The desire to provide polished entertainment for stadium crowds and the national television audience led to professionalization of cheerleading dance groups. The desire for beneficial publicity to promote the parent team led to strict control of cheerleaders' conduct. An examination of profes-sionalization and control in professional cheerleading reveals precedents and parallels with school and college cheerleading.

Professionalization has affected both the cheerleaders and the staff who manage them. As Bruce Chadwick noted, "Today's cheerleaders are as professional at their sport as the players are at football. Like Broadway dancers, they audition for their jobs. . . . They rehearse four to sixteen hours per week . . . are trained by seasoned choreographers, and belong to organizations run as smoothly as most major corporations."[103] Professionalization formalized organizational structures, selection criteria, conditions of employment, and codes of behavior and institutionalized corporate control of all aspects of cheerleading in professional sports.

When the Dallas Cowboys professionalized their cheerleading group in 1972, they hired a Broadway choreographer to replace the schoolteacher who had served as director. The choreographer selected trained dancers to replace the high school volunteers. When the Dallas cheerleaders became nationally known in 1976, the demand for off-field appearances necessitated adding a business manager. At first Suzanne Mitchell served as manager in addition to her job as Tex Schramm's secretary. After two years Mitchell worked full time as manager and eventually was named vice president and director of the cheerleaders.[104] As the Dallas cheerleaders' celebrity and commercial success increased, so did corporate regulation of all aspects of the cheerleaders' behavior. Conditions of employment, standards of physical appearance, and rules for personal and social conduct were outlined in detailed written regulations for the cheerleaders to follow. When other NFL teams formed Dallas-style dance groups, they also adopted many of Dallas's organizational and procedural practices.

Professionalization usually means business managers and choreographers hired by the parent team. The Kansas City Chiefs took professionalization literally by contracting with the International Cheerleading Foundation to direct their squad. ICF employee Susie Walker served as assistant director of the cheerleaders and also performed as a cheerleader on the squad.[105]

Corporate sponsorship outside the parent team is an additional aspect of organizational control in professional cheerleading. During its three-year existence the Pony Express was sponsored jointly by the Denver Broncos and television station KBTV.[106] In 1978 most of the Canadian football teams had corporate sponsors, some of whom provided as much as $20,000 to subsidize the expense of maintaining cheerleading groups.[107]

As with any organization, there are conflicts and disputes between staff and management. Complaints about nepotism, favoritism, and heavy-handed control have been made. In 1990 and 1992 Washington's Redskinettes complained to Redskins management about the husband and wife who directed the cheerleaders, managed squad finances, and hired their daughter (also a Redskinette) as choreographer.[108] Denver Pony Express members complained about managerial favoritism in the selection of cheerleaders to appear in an episode of *Mork and Mindy*.[109]

Suzette Scholz described Suzanne Mitchell's punishing treatment of Dallas cheerleaders who fell out of the director's favor. Mitchell would designate such cheerleaders as "alternates," which meant they could not perform at games, but would have to suit up and remain isolated in the dressing room during entire games.[110] Squad managers could take advantage of the fact that cheerleaders had little bargaining power. For any cheerleader who protested, there were dozens—even hundreds—of women eager to take her place on the squad.

While the external rewards for professional cheerleaders can be considerable, their actual conditions of employment are extremely demanding and restrictive. Nearly every aspect of a cheerleader's behavior is subject to organizational control. This continues to be the case more than twenty years after Dallas established its prototype dance group.

There is frequent turnover among professional cheerleaders and no presumed job security. In rigorous selection and audition processes, veterans must requalify and compete against newcomers each year. Pay is minimal and perks are often modest. Some teams give cheerleaders tickets to home games, but not all teams do so. The primary financial benefits come from personal appearances, and policies for disbursement vary widely among teams. Suzette Scholz noted that Dallas cheerleaders could earn additional money for personal appearances, but were never compensated for cheerleader-endorsed merchandise sold by the Cowboys organization.[111]

Cheerleaders usually must sign contracts which restrict their appearances to events approved by the parent team and prohibit being photographed for publication without permission from the team. They may be required to waive liability for job-related injury. Women preparing to dance at auditions for the New Jersey Generals were advised: "The floor is slippery, so be careful. And be sure you've signed your injury waivers."[112] They were asked to forego claims even before they were employed.

Although they do not perform tumbling and gymnastic stunts common in collegiate and school cheering, professional cheerleaders and their employers face health and injury concerns. Regulations for Philadelphia's Liberty Belles are typical of management's restrictions: "Any girl becoming pregnant must notify us immediately and may continue to cheer until the end of the third month with a doctor's note and as long as her weight does not become a factor."[113] Safety and physical appearance seem to warrant equal concern on the part of management. Jeanie Cavett, eight months pregnant when she successfully tried out for the Dallas Cowboys Cheerleaders in 1978, is an apparent exception to restrictions normally imposed due to liability concerns.[114] Dehydration is a problem when cheerleaders perform for hours in stadiums where the temperature at ground level can exceed 120 degrees. Dallas cheerleaders were forbidden to drink water during strenuous rehearsals in order to "acclimate" them to the heat in Texas Stadium. As a consequence, some would pass out or suffer cramps from dehydration during practice.[115]

Although all professional dancers risk injuries in rehearsal and performance, many football cheerleaders cope with the additional hazard of artificial turf. Like the players, cheerleaders complain that the hard, unresilient surface increases trauma to joints. Susie Walker, cheerleader for the Kansas City Chiefs, said: "Astroturf is the one thing I can do without. We jump and land, jump and land, and our knees and ankles really take a beating. You don't realize what it's like until you are on it."[116]

Like many popular performers, professional cheerleaders have to be wary of physical assault by overenthusiastic fans. Dallas cheerleaders never dance in public appearances outside of games unless they are guaranteed a stage elevated above the audience. This restriction resulted from "harrowing experiences" when crowds pushed and shoved to get at the dancers, or grabbed at their hair and clothing for "souvenirs."[117]

In a more unusual incident, a cheerleader for the Chicago Bulls was hurt by a fellow performer. In 1991 Kimberly Smith filed suit against Ted Giannoulas, the mascot known professionally as The Famous Chicken, claiming that he "broke her jaw and elbow when he tackled her during a game." Giannoulas allegedly grabbed Smith while she was performing a dance routine and threw her to the floor, causing her injuries.[118] Mascots typically perform as clowns, doing stunts and bits of stage business on the sidelines while a game is in progress. The Chicago incident is ironic. The unspoken message of the cheerleaders' performance, "Look but don't touch," is intended for the audience, but the person who violated that convention is himself a performer, not one of the spectators.

One of the most typical conditions of employment for professional cheerleaders is the degree of control exercised by management over their behavior and their image. This control is evident in elaborate regulations, disciplinary sanctions, and policies which maintain a "wholesome but sexy" image for cheerleader groups. Teams regulate their cheerleaders' behavior while maximizing their symbolic allure to a mass audience.

Directors of cheerleading troupes often rule with an iron hand. A boot camp atmosphere prevails in some organizations where cheerleaders are expected to receive instructions and criticism without argument. Dallas Cowboys Cheerleaders must "address superiors with a bright 'Yes, ma'am' or 'Thank you, ma'am'" when spoken to.[119] All squads stress mandatory attendance at rehearsals and games. One missed rehearsal usually bars the cheerleader from performing at the next game. Two missed practices can lead to dismissal from the squad.

Cheerleaders endure numerous regulations about their physical appearance, both on and off the field. Weight restrictions are outlined in written rules and enforced with weekly weigh-ins and public reprimands. Dallas director Suzanne Mitchell ordered a cheerleader, who, at size four, stood five feet, five inches and weighed 109 pounds, to "drop five."[120] Suzette Scholz described how Dallas cheerleaders, frantic to maintain the extreme thinness Mitchell required, abused diet pills, diuretics, and laxatives. Some Dallas cheerleaders used cocaine as an energy booster in lieu of food calories to sustain their strenuous dance workouts.[121] Philadelphia's Liberty Belles and Washington's Redskinettes also had weekly weigh-ins. A Liberty Belle over her weight limit was barred from performing until she lost the prescribed amount. Redskinettes were allowed a three-pound fluctuation for menstrual bloating over their individually assigned weights, but were benched after two warnings if they exceeded that limit.[122]

Other aspects of personal appearance are regulated as well. Redskinettes were strongly encouraged to use hair-weaves to obtain the voluminous style preferred for the squad, and they could not change their hairstyle without the director's approval. Redskinettes were required to wear full makeup at practices because photographers were usually present.[123] In contrast to the uniformity of the Redskinettes, Dallas cheerleaders were selected to provide a variety of "looks." Yet they also could not change their individual hairstyles once they became members of the troupe. Stephanie Scholz wore a fake ponytail for three years as a Dallas cheerleader because the director wanted to differentiate her from sister Suzette who was also on the squad. Each girl was to appeal to a different segment of the audience:

> There was the long-haired blonde, the girl with the
> ponytail, the pigtail girl, the tall brunette, the perky little
> brunette, the bouncy blonde, the sultry redhead, the
> freckle-faced strawberry blonde, the African-American
> girl, the Asian girl, the short girl, the tall girl . . . so
> many different types that just about everybody's fantasy
> could be fulfilled.[124]

Even the cheerleader dolls marketed by the Dallas Cowboys
reflected diverse looks—available in African-American, brunette,
and blonde models. The Redskinettes' director enforced
homogeneity while Dallas's enforced diversity. Both
organizations subordinated the cheerleader's individuality to
images prescribed for the group.

Professional cheerleaders typically face restrictions about
their comportment off the field, since they are viewed as
representatives of the parent franchise even when they are off
duty. In 1990 Redskinette regulations stated: "Appearing in public
with no makeup and stringy hair while wearing your Redskinette
jacket or necklace is inappropriate." Squad members were
prohibited from "using profanity, smoking, chewing gum,
drinking alcohol or using drugs" when wearing items that
identified them as Redskinettes.[125] Rules in the 1980s for Dallas
cheerleaders were more stringent. Since they were individually
recognized as local celebrities, they were required to "look perfect
all the time," when shopping, doing personal errands, and so
forth.[126] This degree of regimentation goes beyond military
discipline, which at least allows for the concept of "off-duty"
civilian behavior. To maintain a corporate image, Dallas Cowboys
Cheerleaders had to be perpetually on Red Alert.

Most clubs have regulations prohibiting fraternization
between cheerleaders and players. The cheerleaders are to be
sexually alluring in the abstract but not in actuality. They are
particularly not to be seen as distractions to the players. Dallas
prohibited dating between cheerleaders and players.[127] The
Oakland Raiders were more lenient, with two exceptions:
Raiderettes were given a list each year indicating which players
were married. Married players were off limits. While Raiderettes
could date single players, they were not permitted to be
"anywhere around the training camp . . . practice field [or] . . .
locker room."[128] In 1985 the Houston Oilers dismissed three
Derrick Dolls for fraternization when they inadvertently attended

a party where some players were present. Although the women left the party immediately, an anonymous caller reported them to management. When the cheerleaders challenged the Oilers in court, fraternization could not be proven, so the Oilers fired them under a clause permitting dismissal "with or without cause."[129]

Every aspect of a professional cheerleader's on-field appearance is dictated by management. Dance routines are planned and selected in advance. No detail is overlooked. Rules for the Liberty Belles stated: "There will be absolutely no smoking, drinking or chewing gum permitted while in uniform. . . . Your appearance must be impeccable at all times. This includes hair, makeup, nails, uniform and shoes."[130] Redskinettes were prohibited from wearing underpants with their uniforms. Panty lines were considered unprofessional. In 1991 a Redskinette was benched for wearing briefs with her costume.[131] Conversely, Dallas Cowboys Cheerleaders were required to wear bras with their uniforms.[132]

The uniforms worn by professional cheerleaders are the most conspicuous aspect of their media image and are more akin to show-girl costumes than to outfits worn by school and college cheerleaders. Cut low to show cleavage, cut high to show thigh, uniforms for professional cheerleaders send a message at odds with the behavioral standards enforced by team officials. The hot-pants uniforms designed for the Dallas cheerleaders in 1972 were an immediate part of their appeal. These provocative uniforms contradict the squeaky-clean propriety which management demands of the cheerleaders.

Dallas was the first team to establish a registered trademark for its cheerleader costume.[133] While other squads have changed uniform designs many times, Dallas has kept its signature costume for more than twenty years. The mystique of the Dallas uniform is reflected in squad rules. Cheerleaders are required to wash their uniforms themselves. Commercial drycleaning or laundry is prohibited lest the uniform get into unauthorized hands. Loss or damage to the uniform is grounds for dismissal from the squad.[134]

When the Washington Redskins announced a change to sexier uniforms for their cheerleaders in 1978 it generated local controversy.[135] Their modest, V-necked, A-line jumpers were replaced by more revealing costumes in an apparent response to the famous Dallas outfits. So many dance groups adopted sexy uniforms that by 1981 Philadelphia opted for a more conservative, collegiate look as a novelty. Liberty Belles director Caroline Cullum outfitted the squad in "angora letter sweaters and pleated skirts," saying she wanted the Belles "to be more like traditional cheerleaders, but still sexy."[136] As always, professional cheerleaders could be wholesome, as long as they were sexually appealing too.

The Liberty Belles' collegiate experiment was an aberration. From the 1970s to the present the norm has been provocative, revealing costumes for professional cheerleaders. During a 1990 NFL preseason game between the Denver Broncos and the Indianapolis Colts, Colts cheerleaders cross-dressed as football players. They wore low-cut, midriff-baring jerseys with team insignia, large shoulder pads, and tight, knee-length spandex pants. White athletic shoes and socks replaced the usual boots. Sporting large pom pons and lacking helmets, the cheerleaders presented an eroticized feminine version of the macho football uniform, an additional spin on typical show-girl costuming.[137]

Professional teams use a variety of devices to define the image of their cheerleading groups and heighten their mystique. Cheerleaders usually perform at home games only, since it is expensive to send troupes of thirty-five to forty dancers to away games. When the Dallas Cowboys played in Super Bowls during the 1970s, their cheerleaders flew in on game day, performed at the game, and were flown home immediately afterwards.[138] While this practice saved on hotel expense, it also served to reinforce an image of the cheerleaders as inaccessible and unattainable objects of fantasy. When Jerry Jones purchased the Cowboys in 1989, corporate policy changed. In 1993 Dallas returned to the Super Bowl after an absence of fourteen years, and the Cowboys Cheerleaders arrived with fanfare three days prior to the game.[139]

It is management policy for Washington Redskinettes to use only their first names in interviews and public appearances.[140] This is done ostensibly for security reasons, but also adds to the Redskinettes' mystique. Redskinettes are prohibited from having their boyfriends or husbands see them off at airports when they travel to personal appearances.[141] There seems to be no purpose for this rule other than promoting an image of the cheerleaders as fantasy objects who have no actual, competing relationships.

In defining their cheerleaders' image, team organizations attempt to maintain a precarious balance between the overtly sexual sell and the rhetoric of respectability. The dilemma of this contradiction is seen in a team's negative reaction when individual cheerleaders pose for *Playboy*, although they are directed to pose suggestively for team posters, calendars, and other promotional materials. The cheerleaders' choreography, costumes, and public appearances are designed to maximize their sexually appealing image, yet their behavior and character are packaged as impeccably wholesome; that is, never actually involving sex.

The promotion of the Dallas Cowboys Cheerleaders is a classic example of this contradictory image manipulation. Each issue of the team's *Dallas Cowboys Weekly* (circulation: 100,000) featured a centerfold photo of a different cheerleader. For these photograph sessions director Suzanne Mitchell would select "something seductive and provocative, the most revealing and sexiest clothes she could find" for the cheerleader to wear. Former cheerleader Suzette Scholz recalled: "It was all part of the big tease. The closer we got to the fans, the more wholesome we were to act and dress. The farther away we got, the more sexually provocative we were made."[142] Mitchell was the same director who established such strict rules of behavior that Dallas cheerleaders could flourish as media heroines in the heart of Southern fundamentalism.

Mitchell retired as cheerleaders director when Jerry Jones purchased the Dallas Cowboys in 1989. Jones created a local furor when he announced that he wanted cheerleaders to act as hostesses at events where liquor was served, that fraternization with players was no longer forbidden, and that new, more revealing costumes (spandex biker shorts and halter tops) would be required. New director Debbie Bond, Mitchell's former assistant, and thirteen members of the squad quit in protest. The irony of the situation was not lost on columnist Molly Ivins, who wrote, "Hard to know what to think when . . . fourteen Dallas Cowboy Cheerleaders have resigned because they believe the team's new owner is trying to make them into sex objects."[143]

The controversy highlighted the contradictory images of nationally known sexpots so sheltered they never appeared at any event where alcohol was served. The cheerleaders' objection to Jones's tampering with their wholesome mystique was matched by public outcry. Just four days after his announcement, Jones reversed himself, saying that "he was influenced by public reaction to the protest retirement."[144] He restored all previous rules for cheerleader comportment and abandoned attempts to change their uniforms.

Adding irony to irony, the Dallas cheerleaders insisted on retaining behavior restrictions which had always been mandated by management. The cheerleaders internalized the wholesome image created for public consumption. As rookie Dallas cheerleader Toni Atwater put it, "I feel like we are a sacred, sacred organization. You can imagine—or, actually you probably can't—the public outpouring of support and sympathy for the cheerleaders."[145] The original sexy-yet-wholesome image created for the Dallas cheerleaders was so well entrenched that a new owner could not trifle with it.

The Dallas Cowboys Cheerleaders are significant in the development of professional cheering because they were the first to combine entertainment and promotion so successfully. They started a phenomenon in professional football which spread to other sports and prompted dozens of imitators. They are still regarded as the standard to emulate more than twenty years after their debut, and they continue to be in demand for public appearances nationwide in the 1990s. Largely because of Dallas's success, professional cheerleading has become an integral part of sports entertainment and marketing.

In 1980 *Denver Post* sportswriter Steve Cameron wrote that the "fad" for "go-go dancers on the sidelines" had "gone its way."[146] The continued presence of cheerleading in professional sport belies Cameron's pronouncement. The Denver Broncos, it should be noted, reestablished a dance troupe in 1993. The sexual sell continues to be an effective marketing device in professional sports, as it is throughout American popular culture.

1. Yell Leader Brandon "Chick" Griffis, Indiana University, 1915. *Arbutus* yearbook photo courtesy of Indiana University Archives.

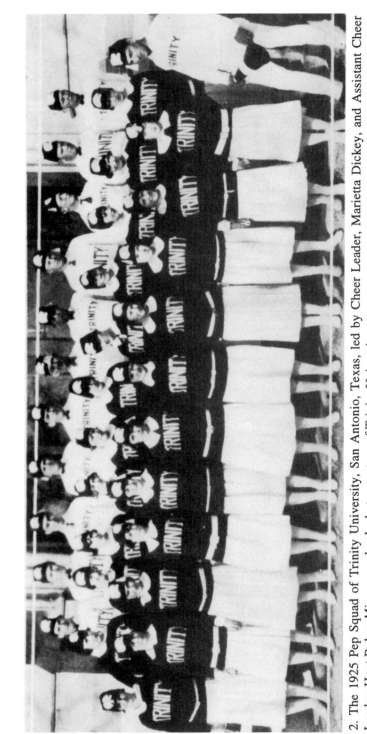

2. The 1925 Pep Squad of Trinity University, San Antonio, Texas, led by Cheer Leader, Marietta Dickey, and Assistant Cheer Leader, Hoyt Boles. *Mirage* yearbook photo courtesy of Trinity University.

3. The 1936 cheerleaders at Trinity University, San Antonio, Texas. Cheer Leader, Elizabeth Jones; assistants, George Newton, *left*, and Howard Rutherford, *right*; and mascot, Serena Ann Wilkins, daughter of Coach L.J. Wilkins. *Mirage* yearbook photo courtesy of Trinity University.

4. The 1937 squad at Trinity University, San Antonio, Texas. Cheer Leader, George Newton; and assistants, Jack Harbin and Dorothy Jo Everheart. *Mirage* yearbook photo courtesy of Trinity University.

5. Cheerleaders of Grossmont Union High School, La Mesa, California, 1944. *Left to right:* Shirley Lorraine Goss, Gerry Kibbey, Doris McAfee. *El Recuerdo* yearbook photo courtesy of Grossmont Union High School.

6. The pom pon squad, Grossmont Union High School, La Mesa, California, 1945. Back row, *left to right:* Helen Eaton, Rae Marie Carr, Elizabeth Noakes, Colleen Campbell. Front row: Marilyn McAfee. *El Recuerdo* yearbook photo courtesy of Grossmont Union High School.

7. University of Denver ice hockey cheerleaders, 1965. *Kynewisbok* yearbook photo courtesy of the University of Denver.

8. A hybrid of school spirit and mass entertainment, the professional cheerleader projects youthful enthusiasm and adult allure. Photo courtesy of Cindy Villerreal-Hughes, Director, Derrick Dolls.

9. Professional cheerleading emphasizes dance and the glamorous sex appeal of performers such as Houston Oilers Derrick Doll Terri Miller. Photo courtesy of Cindy Villerreal-Hughes, Director, Derrick Dolls.

10. Professional cheerleading uniforms have evolved from collegiate-style sportswear to showgirl costumes. The costume of this cheerleader, Zondria Jackson of the Derrick Dolls, combines athletic and theatrical styles. Photo courtesy of Cindy Villerreal-Hughes, Director, Derrick Dolls.

11. The costume worn by Derrick Doll Patty Pascavage exemplifies professional cheerleading's showgirl style. Photo courtesy of Cindy Villerreal-Hughes, Director, Derrick Dolls.

12. Greg Evans's cartoon exemplifies the stereotype of the gorgeous, but conceited, cheerleader. Reprinted with special permission of North America Syndicate.

13. Henry Payne's editorial cartoon reflects the stereotype of cheerleader as inconsequential follower, the opposite of a dynamic player-quarterback. Henry Payne reprinted by permission of United Feature Syndicate, Inc.

14. This cartoon by Don Addis refutes the cheerleader-follower stereotype. When sport moves to mass media show business, the cheerleader gains equal or top billing with players. Reprinted by permission of Don Addis and Creators Syndicate, Inc.

15. Tom Batiuk illustrates the irony of boosting when there is little left to boost—the cheer equivalent of spin control. Reprinted with special permission of North America Syndicate.

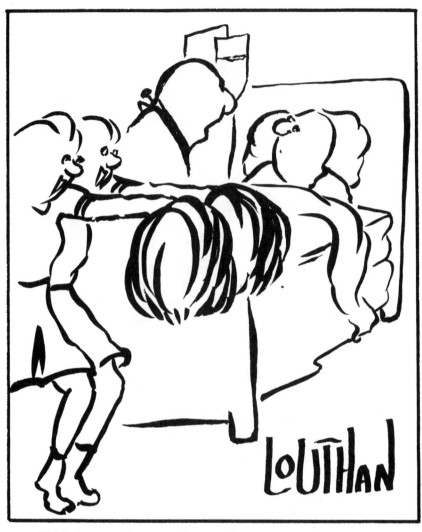

**"We're going to be using a combination
of chemotherapy and 'push em back,
push em back, waaaay back.'"**

16. John Louthan's image can be read as an extension of the frivolous
cheerleader-booster role, or as affirmation of the cheerleader's optimistic,
supportive role. Reprinted by permission of John Louthan.

4

Content and Style:
Spirit, Entertainment, and Competition

Cheerleading has evolved to fulfill a variety of roles in school, community, and mass market contexts. Both content and style have changed over time as cheerleading diversified to serve spirit, entertainment, and competitive functions at the collegiate and scholastic level.

Change has occurred in cheerleader roles and qualifications, performance style, yells, and uniforms. Two important trends have influenced cheering content and style: the specialization of spirit groups (drill teams, dance teams, and mascots) to maximize entertainment, and the emphasis on athleticism and formal competition to establish cheerleading as a sport. These issues relate to cheerleading's transition from an informal demonstration of spectator enthusiasm to a well-rehearsed, physically demanding performance done by specialists.

Spirit and Support

The original aim of the volunteer yell leader was to help his team win by providing rousing verbal support during games. From the beginning, team sports have been the primary focus for organized cheering. Frank Gradler, in 1927, stressed the importance of the cheerleader and rooters to "the winning of the games" in football, basketball, and baseball.[1] Cheering for football and basketball teams is most common today, but sports such as wrestling, soccer, and ice hockey also receive support from cheerleading squads. In today's schools, with multiple sports, varsity and junior varsity teams, and girls' as well boys' teams, considerable demands are placed on cheerleaders' time. Some schools address this by fielding both varsity and junior varsity cheerleading squads or naming separate cheering squads for each major sport.[2]

The college yell leader's direct role during games was soon extended to promoting enthusiasm at supporting events such as pep rallies. At the scholastic level this aspect of the cheerleader's role was strongly emphasized as the promotion of "school spirit" in various activities. In 1945 Newt Loken described the cheerleader as a "central figure" in "occasions for generating high-pitched enthusiasm among the team members and well-wishing students," including rallies, send-offs, and welcome-home receptions.[3] It is now becoming common for cheerleaders to support nonathletic competitions, such as speech tournaments and academic decathlons, as well.[4]

The cheerleader's basic function relates closely to that of the early yell leader:

> the main responsibility of a cheerleader is to raise morale and spirit in the crowd and athletic team. At pep rallies (assemblies designed to promote athletic endeavors and pride) and athletic contests, the cheerleaders lead songs and cheers (short snappy word sequences that people can shout in unison). They signal when the crowd should yell with vocal commands and big arm and body motions.[5]

Cheer manuals stress the cheerleader's responsibility to select yells appropriate to the course of the game in progress and to remain subordinate to the game itself. Bruce Turvold wrote in 1948: "Make sure that, while the game is in progress, the attention of the crowd is centered on it, and not on the cheerleaders." Turvold suggested using a fight yell "when the game is close" and a loyalty or fight yell "when your team is behind."[6] Marylou and Ron Humphrey, in 1970, echoed this theme: "If victory appears certain, drop the fight yells and chants of 'We Want More' nature and switch to school-spirit cheers that praise your team and school." Conversely, "If it appears that you will lose the game . . . drop cheers that mention victory or win. Use school-spirit and fight cheers that call on your team to do its best."[7]

Newt Loken listed appropriate times to lead yells and inappropriate times which would interfere with the game's action. "Appropriate times" included time-outs, breaks between quarters or halves, and a cheer "for that man" when a player was injured. Times not to yell included "when the two teams are in action," and during announcements made on the public address system.[8] Chants of "We want a touchdown" or "Hold that line" were to be made at relevant points in the offensive or defensive action of the game.

This advice was based on the assumption that cheering was secondary to the athletic contest. Frank Gradler warned his reader, "Don't be a clown or a jester. . . . you are not there to entertain and never, under any circumstances, attempt to amuse your crowd by your motions."[9] Newt Loken, writing twenty years later, was more tolerant of "'horse-play' and mirth-provoking antics" to keep crowds "alert, responsive, and in good humor." Loken cautioned, however, that "it is not the purpose of the cheerleader to 'steal the show' from the team."[10]

While early manuals counseled cheerleaders to defer to the events of a game, they were not to defer to the crowd. Cheerleaders were instructed to choose yells to maintain control of the crowd and quash any unsportsmanlike behavior. Gradler cited "the increased complications of handling crowds" as part of the cheerleader's responsibilities.[11] Loken noted that "in case of booing . . . it becomes the duty of the cheerleader to try to silence the offenders."[12] Humphrey and Humphrey advised that "booing must be stopped instantly" and directed cheerleaders to "drown out the boos with your loudest yell or chant." They also cautioned, "Something is wrong when the students start their own cheers or chants. . . . If their cheers are in poor taste, ignore them or drown them out with a regular yell. Do not let the students run the show."[13] Ironically, the original yell leaders did just that; as students they "ran the show" by leading cheers from the stands.

The emphasis on crowd control stemmed from expectations that cheerleaders would promote sportsmanship in student behavior. Cheer manuals from the 1920s to the present stress the demonstration of sportsmanship, which Humphrey and Humphrey define as "the ability to accept defeat without complaint, victory without bragging, and to treat your opponents with fairness and courtesy."[14] Yell selection, the cheerleader's responsibility, was one way to demonstrate sportsmanship. Gradler, in the 1920s, urged avoidance of yells designed "to hurt the morale of the opponents rather than to increase that of the home team."[15] This theme continued with Loken's advice in the 1980s, "All yells should be positive. Boost your team but do not knock the other team."[16]

Cheerleaders at the scholastic level in particular were expected to demonstrate personality and character traits appropriate to their roles as student leaders. Educators saw peer examples in extracurricular activity as a means to influence student behavior in general and set cheerleader qualifications accordingly. At the college level, the yell leader was not seen in such a didactic role, so qualifying tended to emphasize charisma and technical skill over character and academic standing.

From the beginning, the prescriptive literature has listed social as well as physical qualifications for cheerleaders. Gradler identified nine "necessary requisites" in 1927:

1. Popularity among students
2. Good moral character
3. Scholastic ability
4. Diplomacy
5. A natural sense of rhythm
6. Some gymnastic ability
7. A loud, clear voice
8. Physical stamina
9. Enthusiasm[17]

These qualities reflected dual roles as student leader and as cheerleader. Moral as well as physical standards were invoked by Gradler: "A cheer-leader is to a certain extent a hero in the eyes of his fellow students. Do all in your power to maintain that impression." Gradler listed rhythm as "the most important" technical qualification, and stressed that cheerleaders should "have some knowledge . . . at tumbling, turning cart-wheels or hand-springs, and know how to leap and jump gracefully."[18] Regarding stamina, Gradler counseled, "It is just as much a duty of a cheer-leader to train and to practice physical exercises as it is for members of a football team." He advised cheerleaders to develop their arms, legs, back, and breathing capacity.[19] Gradler's emphasis on gymnastic ability and athletic training was directed at college and school yell leaders, nearly all of whom, in the 1920s, were male.

By 1945 Newt Loken's manual addressed female as well as male cheerleaders. He recommended the following qualifications for cheerleaders:

1. Pleasing personality . . . the most important considera-tion . . . [including] pep . . . poise, and confidence
2. Good personal appearance
3. Imagination and resourcefulness
4. Organizing ability and leadership

5. Acrobatic ability . . . a cartwheel should be the minimum requirement
6. A commanding voice[20]

Loken's criteria appear to stress the cheerleader's performance role more than the role of student leader, The characteristics listed by Marylou and Ron Humphrey in 1970 follow this trend. The Humphrey manual states that cheerleaders, both male and female, should "show leadership ability, public-speaking ability, a basic knowledge of game rules, and they should have coordination, a good sense of rhythm, physical strength, and agility."[21] The Humphreys stressed attitudes which cheerleaders should exhibit: "Every cheerleader must show self-confidence all the time—at school, at rallies, and at games." The cheerleader should "watch the game without becoming so emotionally involved that you cannot do a good job of cheer-leading." The original yell leader's expression of spontaneous emotion had become a calculated presentation which required the cheerleader to curb his or her emotions in the line of duty.

The concept of cheerleading as disciplined performance was well established by the 1920s. Prescribed motions, techniques, and cheers were taught and written about, not only to intensify crowd yells, but also to entertain the crowd beyond the action of the game itself. Conventions such as uniformity and precision, and visual as well as verbal action, persist to the present.

Many of the fundamentals outlined in the early manuals are applicable to contemporary cheering. Newt Loken prescribed "general cheerleading motions" which would sound familiar to today's practitioners: "Use wide, sweeping movements . . . easily followed from a distance. Keep hands open, and arms straight. . . . [L]ook toward the crowd throughout a yell. . . . Animate as many cheers as possible with flips, rolls, and handsprings."[23] Bruce Turvold stressed uniformity: "The first thing to do in creating a good cheerleading squad is to train the members to keep together . . . as nearly alike as possible. No one . . . should be a show-off. They should agree on a single system of motions, jumps, and yells, which the entire squad should use."[24] Decades later, Marylou and Ron Humphrey continued the emphasis on precision, uniformity, sharp motions, and eye contact: "When performing, there is just one position for the head—toward the spectator. Even when the body is facing or moving sideways, look over your shoulder at the spectators."[25]

Tumbling and lifts to build formations became part of collegiate cheerleading when all cheerleaders were male. Gymnastic elements made yell leaders more visible in large stadiums and added to the spectacle of athletic performance occurring on the field of play. Randy Neil described the rationale for cheering gymnastics: "Crowd control is often based on first getting the attention of your fans . . . then having them do the cheers. . . . Since the beginning of active cheerleading . . . pepsters have used stunts and acrobatics to spark up their routines with 'attention-getting' devices."[26]

The tradition of athletic tumbling was adopted by school cheerleaders and continued to influence scholastic cheering in its later coeducational and feminized versions. Neil, citing the University of Florida's coeducational squad as "Number One Innovators of mounts, lifts and pyramids," noted that the athletic style of partner stunts was "sweeping America" in the mid-1970s.[27] Another trend beginning in the 1970s was the use of mini-trampolines to produce "spectacular jumps and high flips."[28] Both male and female cheerleaders did these stunts.

Athletic elements added entertainment value, but the central focus of cheerleading in game situations continued to be the yells. The cheerleader's primary role was to synchronize and intensify audience response with designated yells. Gradler characterized the cheerleader's function as "similar to that of a band or orchestra director whose task it is to bring each instrument in perfect time and harmony with the music. The words and the rhythm of the cheer are your music."[29]

The wording of cheers varies to reflect current slang and regional, ethnic, and local school culture, but basic types of cheers have remained constant since the early 1900s. The *fight* cheer is simple and direct:

> Fight, Raiders!
> Go, Raiders!
> Fight, fight, FIGHT!

The *novelty* cheer involves audience action as well as words:

> Clap your hands (clap, clap, clap)
> Stamp the floor (stamp, stamp, stamp)
> Go, Blue Demons, Raise that score!

The *call and response* cheer alternates between cheerleaders and spectators:

What do we want?	Victory
Say it again	Victory
Louder!	VICTORY!

The *locomotive* cheer spells out school or team names, slowly at first, then increasing speed with repetitions.[30] The Princeton locomotive is thought to be the first recorded college yell:

Ray, Ray, Ray,
Tiger, Tiger, Tiger,
Sis, Sis, Sis,
Boom, Boom, Boom,
Aaaaaaaaah!
Princeton, Princeton, Princeton!

Newt Loken notes that this cheer "was suggested by a rouser of the Seventh Regiment of New York City, and was picked up by undergraduates who gathered at the railroad station when the Regiment went through Princeton en route to Washington at the outbreak of the Civil War."[31] Princeton graduate Thomas Peebles brought the cheer and the sport of football to the University of Minnesota in 1884. In 1885 John W. Adams and Win Sargent created the "famous and still-used yell, 'Rah, Rah, Rah! SKI-U-MAH, MINN-E-SO-TA!'"[32]

Some early college yells incorporated literary and mathematical allusions to undergraduate studies. According to Charles Kuralt's survey of old-time cheers, the Yale cheer, "Brekekekex, Ko-ax, Ko-ax!" was derived "from the croaking chorus of *The Frogs* by Aristophanes." The California Institute of Technology contributed:

Secant, cosine, tangent, sine,
Logarithm, logarithm, hyperbolic sine,
Three-point-1-4-1-5-9,
Slip stick, slide rule,
Tech, Tech, Tech![33]

Secondary schools borrowed and adapted college yells. In 1927 Gradler observed that some cheers "long ago lost their origin and have become the general property of a great number of schools." He urged cheerleaders, "Strive to create at least one good cheer characteristic of your school."[34]

Originality in developing cheers was encouraged, but cheerleaders were advised not to use objectionable yells which advocated violence or showed disrespect for opponents. Bruce Turvold cited as examples to avoid: "Smash 'em, bust 'em, That's our custom," and

> Go back, go back, go back to the woods,
> You haven't, you haven't, you haven't got the goods,
> You haven't got the rhythm, and you haven't got the jazz,
> You haven't got the team that Central has![35]

These caveats were consistent with expectations that cheerleaders would maintain crowd control and promote good sportsmanship. It must be noted, however, that cheers invented and transmitted by spectators have always existed along with "authorized" cheers. Such cheers tend to be less polite (and more amusing) than orthodox yells. They enter the public domain and are claimed by various schools. Northwestern University's consolation cheer, also attributed to the University of Chicago, is a good example. Northwestern football fans, mired in a 31-game losing streak in the early 1980s, are credited with chanting to victorious opponents from large, state universities:

> That's all right,
> That's OK,
> They're gonna work for us someday![36]

Most cheers were adopted from compilations and manuals or transmitted informally via oral tradition. With the rise of clinics and camps, entrepreneurs developed yells which participants then took back to their schools. All of these mechanisms continue to operate today.

The verbal content of cheering has remained relatively stable from the Princeton locomotive to the present. Time limitations during games and the need for crowd response dictate short, simple phrasing and measured delivery. Cheering style, however, is susceptible to changes influenced by popular culture.

In the 1960s and early 1970s, soul music, based in black gospel and rhythm and blues, gained wide appeal in mainstream pop music and dance. This black culture influence extended to cheerleading as well. Eddie Anderson, a black cheerleader elected head yell leader at UCLA in 1966, is credited with introducing soul yells and soul dancing to collegiate cheering in California.[37] In 1971 the *New York Times* reported that "one of the few new wrinkles in cheerleading in recent years has been the addition of soul yells to the cheering repertoires of both all-white and integrated high schools." Pamela Dinkins, a black cheerleading captain at Hempstead (Long Island) High School, said, "We like the kind of cheers where you can stand up in the stands and dance."[38]

By 1972 cheer entrepreneur Lawrence Herkimer had incorporated "Rhythm and Soul Cheers and Chants" into the material taught at his camps.[39] Typical soul yells included:

> We got the super soul spirit,
> We got the SSS!
>
> S-O-U-L, Soul team,
> Sock it to me now![40]

The dancing, jiving rhythm and motion of soul cheering differed from the straight-arm style and standardized cadence of mainstream cheerleading. From "rhythm-nastic" cheering in the 1940s to jazz and hip hop in the present, contemporary dance forms have influenced cheerleading style.

As cheerleading became formalized, uniforms became a conspicuous aspect of performance. Initially, male yell leaders, as members of the crowd, wore street attire at games—frock coats, derby hats, and so forth. By the early twentieth century, designated cheering squads were the norm. Men wore a version of casual street clothes distinguished by school colors or insignia, and the convention of a uniform was established. Their matching outfits helped to focus crowd attention and "create an appearance of unity within the squad."[41] Frank Gradler's 1927 manual advised cheerleaders to "avoid any fantastic costumes or grotesque garbs." He noted that "white duck trousers and a sweater in your school's colors always make a good uniform. It is also well to have a letter or monogram of your school on your sweater."[42] This uniform was well established by the 1930s and 1940s, but Gradler's caution was not universally heeded. Ralph Shoenstein, in a *Saturday Evening Post* essay, recalled his boyhood awe at Dartmouth's cheerleaders in the 1940s: "Only one group of cheerleaders ever made me widen my eyes. . . . Dressed like Indians, they were bare to the waist in twenty degrees, while Brown and Cornell were exhorted by chests that were warmed by Abercrombie and Fitch."[43] From the 1940s to the present, the majority of men's cheerleading uniforms have resembled casual street clothes—slacks, and a sweater, jersey, or polo shirt. Recent variations include warmup suits and the substitution of shorts for slacks. The latter introduces a measure of gender parity, since women's cheer uniforms usually feature very short skirts.

When women entered cheerleading, their uniforms also resembled street clothes—sweaters or blouses, plus full or pleated skirts which mirrored contemporary style and length. In the 1920s and 1930s, uniform skirts were at or below knee-length.[44] In 1945 Newt Loken observed, "Girls truly 'get the breaks' in the matter of diversity and eye appeal of cheerleading apparel," in contrast to male cheerleaders' "more conservative" white flannels and sweaters.[45] Throughout the 1940s women's outfits included princess-style dresses, jumpers, and satin culotte and jacket sets, as well as skirt and sweater combinations. Slacks were sometimes worn in cold weather.

Early manuals stressed neatness and uniformity of dress for males. By the 1940s, instructions for females stressed propriety. Turvold stated, "A cheerleader is conspicuous enough without making herself more so. Her skirt should be no shorter than the knee-length street dress. Tights are a necessity."[46] Interestingly, most of the squad photographs in Turvold's book show girls in mid-thigh skirts, bare legs, and ankle socks.

In the 1950s cheerleading skirts lengthened considerably, following contemporary fashion. By the 1960s short skirts became common in women's cheer uniforms. A similar trend occurred in women's golf and tennis dresses. The advent of miniskirts in the late 1960s made cheerleading outfits look somewhat conservative by comparison. In 1983, Loken advised, "Skirts should reach no lower than the middle of the kneecap."[47] Cheer uniforms with short skirts continue to be the norm.

Accessories have not changed much over the years. Oxfords were worn at first; tennis shoes came later. Saddle shoes became popular in the 1940s and continued to be into the 1960s. The widespread adoption of athletic shoes by cheerleaders in the

1970s reflected current fashion. At present, specialized cheerleading shoes are advertised which have finger grips to facilitate overhead lifts.[48]

The use of megaphones and pom pons seems to be restricted by gender. While girls sometimes use megaphones, this accessory has been identified with male cheerleaders since its introduction by University of Minnesota yell leaders in 1898.[49] Boys never use pom pons, which have been associated with girl cheerleaders and song leaders since the 1940s. Gradler advised male cheerleaders regarding megaphones: "If you do find it necessary to use such an aid, use a large one and never appear before a crowd with these small, miniature affairs that rah-rah boys in movies use."[50] Crepe paper pom pons were in use by West Coast high school girls in the 1940s.[51] Always fragile, and prone to bleed color in rain or snow, paper pom pons were widely used until vinyl equivalents, the "first major equipment innovation in the field," were introduced by the International Cheerleading Foundation in 1968.[52]

Nathan Joseph and Nicholas Alex note that any uniform "acts as a totem, reveals and conceals statuses, certifies legitimacy, and suppresses individuality."[53] These functions apply to cheering uniforms, which provide a focus for school identity and signify the wearer's status as leader and performer. It is customary for school cheerleaders to wear their uniforms to class on game days. This promotes the event among students, and promotes the cheerleaders as well. Because uniforms represent an institution, the behavior of cheerleaders while in uniform is regulated. Observers can identify with the school which cheerleaders represent, but the uniforms also identify the cheerleaders as a group apart from the general crowd. Beyond status and symbolism, the uniforms continue to add color and animation to cheering performance.

Entertainment

Collegiate athletics evolved from in-group events, solely for students, to spectator sports with community, regional, and mass appeal. In the context of sport as recreational diversion for an audience, spirit groups—yell leaders, cheerleading squads, flashcard rooter sections, song girls, drill teams, and mascots—provide entertainment beyond the drama of athletic contests themselves.

The impulse to entertain began with the early yell leaders who added tumbling and acrobatics to focus audience attention on the cheers. The pageantry of marching bands provided music to which song girls and drill teams performed. Flash-card groups and costumed mascots presented additional visual diversions for large crowds which were distant from the field of play. The proliferation of spirit groups created more activities for students to participate in and reinforced the expectation that sports would provide a "show" as well as a "contest."

Of the various types of spirit groups, cheerleaders are most directly involved in the events of the game. They select yells to rally support or signify success at crucial junctures. They help interpret the progress of the game to the crowd and elicit responses which are intended to benefit the team as it plays the game. Other spirit groups, in contrast, perform independently of the game's action, during halftime or in pregame ceremonies. Drill teams and song girls (dance groups) perform long, set routines to music. Their performances, like those of flash-card sections, are visual, requiring full attention of the audience to be appreciated.

As cheering style evolved to maximize entertainment value, it has become more performance oriented and less subordinate to the athletic events which provided its original context. Cheerleading was quick to incorporate visual elements to enhance its verbal function. Ironically, visual elements, such as unison, precision, multiple formations, tumbling, lifts, and pyramid-building, called attention to cheerleading as a performance separate from the performance of the athletes on the field. Continuing emphasis on the visual appeal of cheerleading has fostered its role as a performing entity beyond its original supportive role.

Cheerleading has stylistic elements in common with other types of spirit groups. Gradler observed that while "bleacher stunts" with flash cards do not increase "the direct support of the team on the field, [they] have desirable influence on the crowd itself."[54] Spectacular acrobatic stunts performed by cheerleaders are analogous in that they capture audience attention, but have no bearing on the outcome of the game in progress.

Cheerleading style uses dance and precision movements identified with song-leader and drill-team groups which perform exclusively to music. Randy Neil notes that song-leader (dance) groups emerged in West Coast universities in the 1930s, with the UCLA Song Girls developing an "extremely complex and sophisticated" style in the 1950s.[55] Song-girl groups perform dance steps and often use pom pons to emphasize arm movements. Their routines are visual in appeal: "Once the band starts, the stage is theirs. They perform for an audience which is there to watch only them."[56] Female cheerleaders use pom pons to accentuate arm motions in cadence with the yell. Male cheerleaders use arm motions or wave megaphones. Cheerleaders, having to compete for the crowd's attention during a game, use some of the dance groups' visual techniques.

Many drill teams use pom pons; others, such as the Apache Belles and Kilgore Rangerettes, perform without them. The emphasis in drill choreography is on "precision and repetition."[57] Large formations and synchronization are elements in the visual appeal of drill-team routines. Like the dance groups, drill teams do not perform during the action of a game. Their numbers last the length of a song and they require more space than the sidelines provide. Cheerleading style borrows elements of drill choreography, including formation changes in which squad members shift in and out of lines, break into smaller groups, and recombine to the full group.

Cheerleading also shares some characteristics with another type of spirit leader, the mascot, a student who appears during games costumed as a manifestation of the team's nickname. Mascots were traditional at some universities by the 1940s. Lawrence Brings's manual, School Yells, contains a photograph of Penn State's "Nittany Lion," in full costume, complete with fangs and paws.[58] Newt Loken described "Oski," the bear mascot of the University of California at Berkeley, who was "often simulated by students dressed in a papier-mâché bear's head, padded yellow sweater, and blue pants, as part of the between-the-halves festivities."[59] In the past twenty years, it has become more common for colleges, schools, and professional teams to use mascots to add comic relief to the spectacle of team sports. In addition to performing skits and pantomiming reactions to the game's events, some mascots also interact with members of the audience, posing for photographs and hugging children, much like characters at Disneyland do. Most mascots are caricatures, humorous, larger-than-life versions of animals, such as UCLA's Joe and Josie Bruin, or humans, such as Wyoming's Cowboy. Others, such as Tulane's Green Wave, manage to personify a more abstract concept. What cheerleaders and mascots have in common is direct communication with the crowd concerning the game in progress. Mascots use pantomime to "comment" on the success or failure of their team, while cheerleaders "comment" via the selection of yells they perform. Both mascots and cheerleaders help to interpret the contest to the audience.

When cheerleaders perform their primary role of supporting the team during play, they must actually compete with the team for the crowd's attention. Less directly, the cheering squad competes for attention with other spirit groups whose performance is designed exclusively to entertain. Cheerleading style, in adopting entertainment techniques, has moved closer to performance. At present, cheerleaders do set routines and acrobatic stunts which are independent of the actions of the game on the field. Squads continue to lead cheers, but they also present highly polished, self-contained performances.

Athleticism

The tradition of athleticism, which required tumbling skill and physical stamina in early male yell leaders, continued as collegiate and scholastic cheering became coeducational or feminized activities. The participation of females who were smaller and lighter than male cheerleaders facilitated stunts such as three-level pyramids, flying tosses, and overhead lifts. Athletic cheerleading done by males and females coexisted with drill- and dance-related styles done by females exclusively.

When gymnastics coach Lee Cunningham became faculty advisor to Georgia's cheerleaders in 1963, he required that male squad members be able to do continuous backflips for 50 yards. Most male participants were also members of Georgia's gymnastics team. Female squad members had to undergo three weeks of training in "tumbling and somersaulting off trampolines" prior to tryouts.[60] Athletic college cheering influenced scholastic style by example and through the efforts of cheer entrepreneurs who, coming from college ranks, taught athletic stunts to school cheerleaders in camps and clinics.

In 1984, *International Gymnast* described the three "most demanding aspects" of cheerleading as: "partner stunts (where the guys throw, catch, and hold the girls), pyramids (when many people mount on top of each other to achieve a formation), and basic tumbling skills."[61] The assumption was that males did the lifting, throwing, and catching. By the 1990s, females were lifting, throwing, and catching other females in highly athletic school cheerleading. The following description of a stunt by the Churchill High School squad of San Antonio, Texas, is indicative:

> Four cheerleaders throw senior Yumi Barthel into the air. She soars towards the rafters in the Churchill High School gym and executes a toe-touch: Legs in a wide V, arms reaching to touch her pointed toes as they pop to the approximate level of her ears. The stunt is called a basket toss: Two girls weave their arms together to make a basket—the springboard that will send Barthel over their heads. A girl in front helps support the basket; another in back helps lift Barthel onto the others' arms for takeoff and catch her when she lands. . . . That Barthel goes that high, that she comes down right into their arms, that they can do this in the time it takes to count 1-2-3-4 is, if not unbelievable, at least impressive.[62]

Rigorous physical conditioning, training, and practice are required to perform athletic cheerleading at this level. Gymnasts have an advantage as cheerleaders, according to *International Gymnast*, since they are "accustomed to hard work and discipline, have better general body awareness, and usually superior body control."[63] At the college level, male cheerleaders prepare by means of weight training for the lifts, throws, and catches they do.[64] During the summer, Churchill High School's female cheerleaders "work in the weight room and run a mile each day for stamina before their two-hour practices." This training enables a 100-pound girl to do a shoulder stand with another 100-pound girl.[65] Athletic cheering style has even influenced drill teams, such as the Kilgore Rangerettes, to add lifts (but not tumbling or throws) to their high-kicks, splits, and dance routines.[66]

As athletic forms of cheering have gained greater emphasis, the incidence of injuries has increased. In 1978 the National Gymnastic Catastrophic Injury Registry was established to document "every permanent neurological injury (spinal cord or cerebral, fatal or nonfatal) in the nation resulting from a gymnastic accident, including cheerleading." Sponsored by the U.S. Gymnastics Safety Association, the registry was developed to help the American Alliance for Health, Physical Education, Recreation and Dance and the National Collegiate Athletic Association assess "preventive measures" such as their "safety guidelines for trampoline and minitramp use in physical education and sport."[67]

From July 1979 through June 1980, four catastrophic injuries were documented, two in gymnastics and two in cheerleading. A high school female, age seventeen, suffered a fractured neck and died after falling from a forward flip off the shoulders of another cheerleader during practice. A collegiate male cheerleader, age twenty, suffered permanent paralysis after fracturing his neck during unscheduled practice while using a minitramp.[68]

The number of such injuries was relatively small, considering the large number of participants, but national concern about cheering safety increased after two serious accidents occurred in 1986. A North Dakota State cheerleader suffered fatal brain injury "when she attempted a dismount from the top of a three-person pyramid onto a bare field-house floor during practice." One month later, a University of Kentucky cheerleader was paralyzed when he did "a forward roll off a minitrampoline and landed on the back of his neck." He was practicing for a non-cheerleading tumbling exhibition at the time of the accident.[69]

In response to concerns that cheer competitions encouraged increasingly dangerous stunts, the National Cheerleaders Association issued safety guidelines in 1987. The NCA barred most types of three-tier pyramids and a "split-catch" partner stunt which caused many cheerleaders to break their noses and forearms when dismounting from an overhead toss. The guidelines required "spotters" to stand in front of and behind two-tier pyramids to help cheerleaders dismount. The guidelines prompted the University of New Mexico to purchase padded floor mats for cheer practice sessions.[70] While the NCA guidelines were binding for its competitions only, they influenced some college and school athletic associations to restrict dangerous stunts. The Western Athletic Conference ruled in July 1987 to prohibit pyramid building, free falls, and catapulting by cheerleaders.[71]

The incidence of non-catastrophic injuries suffered by cheerleaders is very high. A 1990 study of hospital emergency room reports conducted by the Consumer Product Safety Commission documented 12,405 injuries attributed to elementary school, high school, and college cheerleading.[72] Sonja Steptoe, describing cheerleading camps, noted the presence of "bandages, casts and leg braces. Crutches, ice packs and empty Advil wrappers litter the workout areas." She observed, "Several times a day the wail of ambulances can be heard. . . . It is a part of camp life."[73]

Even if cheerleaders do not perform risky athletic stunts, cheering makes them susceptible to physical and vocal injuries.

Injuries to the hand and wrist, including nerve compression, ganglion cysts, and torn cartilage, are typical.[74] Paul Bravender's study of the effects of cheerleading on the female singing voice found that cheering for three or more years "results in a statistically higher incidence of severe dysfunction," including "a high degree of hoarseness and the inability to phonate throughout the full compass of the normal female voice." Bravender concluded that "females who are interested in using their voices for singing should refrain from cheerleading."[75] He observed that the cheerleader's main function (yelling) actually constitutes "vocal abuse," which speech pathologists define as "overuse, in terms of duration, force, and range [and] faulty techniques of sound production." Bravender recommended that effects on the male singing voice also be studied, and noted that only Newt Loken, in his 1961 manual, *Cheerleading,* 2nd ed., gave instructions for "proper vocal technique" and resting the voice when strained."[76] Monica McHenry and Alan Reich also studied "vocally abusive behaviors" contributing to the "disproportionately large number of high school cheerleaders [who] develop vocal dysfunction."[77] Cheerleading, whether athletic or vocal in emphasis, poses risks to participants.

Competition

The promotion of competitive cheerleading by the entrepreneurial associations has strongly influenced cheering style. Bob Anderson's 1975 survey of cheerleading contrasted the "sophisticated, structured, and stylized" form of competitive cheerleading with the "simplicity of short, big-crowd cheers." He noted that competitive cheerleading had moved "off the field and on stage."[78] Cheer associations sponsored national competitions for college squads in the 1970s. These contests have been televised annually since 1978, giving additional impetus to an athletic style which demands strength, agility, and speed.[79] Cheer promoters have extended regional and national competitions to the secondary school level as well. In December 1992, the National Cheerleaders Association sponsored "the largest high school cheerleading championship ever," a two-day event in San Antonio, Texas, which drew more than 7,000 competitors in 558 squads from thirty-nine states.[80]

For competition, squads perform four-minute routines combining lifts, tumbling, catches, pyramids, and formation changes done at a rapid pace. The Bernalillo (New Mexico) High

School squad, which qualified for national competition in 1989, described speed as its specialty: "You'll see a 3-level formation (one on the floor, one standing and one on shoulders or above) and in an instant it all changes. We do it so quickly that most people can't figure out how we got into it. That's our strong point."[81]

Competitions are performed before judges and a crowd of several thousand spectators. Judges consider several criteria: "The difficulty of the routine, how precise the group is, if the routine is original in composition and balanced in variety (includes formation changes, jumps, stunts, etc.). . . . The charisma of the group is very important . . . [including its] personality and projection."[82] Judging is more subjective than in other performance sports such as diving or gymnastics, since there are no set deductions for errors, missed stunts, and so forth.[83]

Cheer camps, held during summer months, tie into the association-sponsored competitions. Squads attending National Cheerleaders Association camps are evaluated on routines they prepare in advance and on new material taught at the camp. Squads judged best all around receive an automatic bid to NCA's national competition. Teams which do not qualify at a camp must compete in regional competitions in order to get a bid to the national contest. Entrepreneurs boost camp attendance by linking it to competitive eligibility. In the process they promote an athletic, competitive cheering style to all camp attendees, most of whom never go to nationals. The cheer associations sponsor competitions for all types of spirit groups, including drill teams and mascots.

In 1945 Newt Loken and Otis Dypwick celebrated cheering for its many elements: "In its present glorification, the art of cheerleading embraces endless skills and talents—acrobatics, gymnastics, pantomime, theatrics, showmanship, pageantry, clowning, dancing, music . . . and on and on."[84] They recognized cheerleading's supportive and entertaining functions, but did not anticipate the evolution of these functions into competitive cheerleading as an end in itself. In some instances, competition eclipses the support role. When Rockville, Maryland's Robert Peary High School pom-pon squad was preparing for a drill team competition in 1974, all practices were held in the school cafeteria and gymnasium. Since the competition would take place before a large audience, the coach wanted to accustom the squad to crowds. He scheduled the squad to perform at halftime during one of Peary High's football games as a dress rehearsal for the drill competition.[85] The original support/entertainment role of a drill team thus became secondary to its competitive role, although this priority was not evident to Peary's football crowd. A more obvious demonstration of priorities took place in 1988 at Adams City High School in Commerce City, Colorado, when most of the cheerleaders failed to show up for a scheduled wrestling meet because it conflicted with their practice session to prepare for a cheer competition.[86] In this case competition took conspicuous precedence over the cheer squad's designated support role.

Sport or Activity?

All cheerleading squads support athletic teams at their respective institutions, but not all squads cheer competitively. Debate continues whether cheerleading should be considered a sport or an activity. The athletic nature of contemporary cheering, which is fostered by camps and competitions, argues for consideration as a sport; yet the continuing perception that cheerleading is a feminine role reinforces the assumption that cheering is a support activity.

The distinction is important, particularly at the scholastic level, because sports are typically funded by the sponsoring institution, while activities are funded by their participants. Schools pay sport expenses for travel, uniforms, medical care, insurance, and coaches; but schools do not necessarily fund the cheer and drill teams which support the sports. Educational policy is mixed. The Albuquerque, New Mexico, public school system, for example, considers cheerleading and drill teams to be activities, while the New Mexico Activities Association, which oversees state-wide interscholastic competition, considers them sports.[87]

The athletic nature of contemporary cheerleading prompted *International Gymnast* to declare it a "contact sport" in which "[t]he greatest amount of impact occurs while performing pyramids and partner stunts."[88] Participants concur. As Regina K. Baker, a varsity cheerleader at Henry Clay High School in Lexington, Kentucky, puts it: "If people watch us, they can see it's a sport. If they don't think it is, I'd like to have them try to do what we do."[89]

In addition to its intrinsic qualifications as a sport, collegiate cheerleading, in particular, has acquired some of the external trappings of competitive sport: televised contests, recruitment of skilled practitioners, scholarships, and salaried coaches. In 1992, more than eighty colleges offered scholarships to cheerleaders, including full-tuition grants at the University of Georgia and the University of Kentucky.[90] Unlike other amateur sports which have been formally organized, cheerleading has no national governing body or uniform rules of competition. Cheer associations, collegiate athletic conferences, and state and local school districts issue their own guidelines for participants, coaches, and judges.[91]

Historically, college and school cheerleaders have sometimes received the kind of awards associated with athletics. Frank Gradler's 1927 manual noted, "In some schools, the importance of a cheer-leader is respected to the extent that he is rewarded with letters and tokens similar to those received by the athletes themselves."[92] A 1971 *New York Times* survey of scholastic cheering reported, "Cheerleading and marching trophies [for majorettes] are highly prized possessions in a school's trophy cabinet, and the girls who win them take what they are doing seriously."[93]

Educational policies regarding cheerleading at the secondary school level are varied. Some educators define cheering as a sport; others maintain it is an activity. In fact, dual roles exist in school systems which organize cheerleading as a competitive sport, since those cheerleaders also perform in support of other sports. In states such as Pennsylvania, interscholastic cheer competition is not permitted. Virginia has recently changed policy. In 1990 the Virginia High School League considered cheerleaders a support group, not a competitive group. Students were permitted to compete in cheer association–sponsored contests as individuals, but they could not compete as representatives of their schools.[94] By 1994, however, school teams could compete in district and regional cheerleading meets established "to mirror the local format for athletic playoffs."[95]

The Pennsylvania Interscholastic Athletic Association does not recognize cheerleading as a sport, which led the York County Interscholastic Association to recommend in 1989 that cheerleaders not be allowed to compete in contests sponsored by non-school agencies either. A parent who supported competitive cheering described the dilemma posed by both associations' restrictions: "Cheerleading's not a sport because they don't compete, and they can't compete because it's not a sport."[96] Administrators at Dover Area High School voted against the county association's recommendation and sent the Dover, Pennsylvania, squad to two out-of-state competitions in 1990.[97]

Other school systems recognize cheerleading as a sport on equal par with other sports. When the *Albuquerque Tribune* reported in 1989 that Eldorado High School of Albuquerque had won three state titles, the school's principal wrote to the sports editor pointing out an oversight: "Eldorado attained four state titles. . . . Not only did Eldorado capture state championships in girls soccer, girls basketball and boys gymnastics, but also a AAAA state title was achieved by the varsity cheerleaders."[98] As part of a 1989 school reorganization in Fayetteville, North Carolina, ninth graders who had attended county schools returned to post schools at Fort Bragg. The addition of ninth graders converted Fort Bragg's middle school into a junior high school, requiring a "full-fledged sports program . . . [to] include basketball, baseball, boys' and girls' track, girls' softball, cheerleading and co-ed soccer," with football and wrestling to be added later. The Fort Bragg School Board approved coaching salaries for the new program, including $490 for a cheerleading coach and $950 for a football coach.[99]

Conflicting attitudes about cheerleading's function are also reflected in school responses to Title IX, which prohibits sex discrimination in interscholastic athletics. In 1977 Janice Kaplan noted that some "traditional" athletic directors and principals made cheerleading a varsity sport rather than create new sports programs for girls: "By giving the girls cheerleading uniforms every year and paying for them to travel with the football team, it looks as if a school is spending money on women's sports."[100] Kaplan assumed that cheering was a supporting activity, done only by females. Conversely, in 1992 cheerleading was cited as a legitimate sport deserving equal treatment as part of a plan to implement Title IX compliance. The Montgomery County, Maryland, Task Force on Gender Equity in Athletics, finding the county not in compliance, called for equitable funding and facilities for girls' and boys' sports, and recommended that cheerleading be recognized as a sport to give cheerleaders "the same rights as every other athlete. . . . What they do is an athletic endeavor. They deserve the same benefits."[101] The Task Force also assumed that cheerleading was done primarily by females, but recognized its physically demanding aspects.

Interestingly, current Title IX provisions address the supportive, rather than the athletic, aspect of cheerleading. Bernice Sandler's interpretation of the effect of Title IX on higher education makes the distinction: "Cheerleading programs are not considered part of athletic programs. . . . Insofar as a cheerleading program is viewed by DOE as *support* provided to an institution's athletic teams, it must be available for men's and women's teams without discrimination."[102]

As cheerleading developed to provide entertainment, to promote sportsmanship, and to become a competitive sport, it became somewhat removed from its original, supporting role. Similarly, the spirit groups which grew out of cheerleading have evolved to emphasize entertainment and competition as well as direct support. In a pattern which has now come full circle, the University of California at Los Angeles announced in 1990 the return of the Yell Crew "to make sure that all Bruin fans get into the act and cheer their lungs out for the team." Yell Crew members, "extroverts all," are chosen for their "charisma and leadership" and "volume of voice."[103] UCLA's mascots, dance team, and acrobatic cheerleaders continue to provide their specialized performances, while the Yell Crew recreates the role of the original yell leaders.

While the content of cheerleading has diversified into specialized forms emphasizing drill, dance, comedy, and acrobatics, each of these elements was present to some degree in the routines of the early yell leaders. The rise of drill teams and dance groups gave female students opportunities to participate in activities deemed appropriately feminine, but for decades young women have also participated in athletically demanding acrobatic cheering. Since the 1970s, competitive cheerleading has provided an athletic outlet for both male and female cheerleaders. The basic function of cheerleading, however, continues to be a support device for other competitors. In this sense, regardless of cheerleader skill or gender, cheering is socially defined as a feminine role. This definition is reinforced by the numeric predominance of female cheerleaders.

Cheering was an exclusively masculine activity when the first college yell leaders emerged—all the students were males and all the athletes were males. When increasing numbers of female students entered colleges and secondary schools and participated as cheerleaders, athletics continued to be defined as a masculine activity. By emphasizing cheerleading's emotionally supportive role, conventional gender behaviors were preserved—males competed, females encouraged. With the enactment of Title IX, athletics are now officially recognized as appropriate feminine behavior. Given these opportunities, and the rise of competitive cheering, it remains to be seen if cheerleading will be redefined as a gender-neutral activity.

5

On the Sidelines and in the Headlines: Images of Cheerleading in American Culture

This chapter title could also include "Plot Lines, Punch Lines, and Product Lines," since representations of the cheerleader are found in every expression of American popular culture. Cheerleader images abound in editorial, advertising, promotional, didactic, and entertainment media. Every participant in American culture has a personal story, comment, or opinion about cheerleaders. They are fixtures in our schools, magazines, newspapers, television, and movies. Judging by the variety of contexts and frequency with which it is used, the cheerleader is an effective, multipurpose symbol.

What does cheerleading, as reflected in popular culture, signify to observers and to cheerleaders themselves? The ubiquitous cheerleader icon reveals both conflict and consensus in cultural values concerning status, youth, competition, success, celebrity, gender, and sexuality. For example, contemporary perceptions of the cheerleader emphasize qualities defined in negative, feminine terms such as vanity and exhibitionism. Yet cheerleading form and style are sanctioned and maintained by institutional and parental definitions of appropriate feminine behavior. Writer Kathleen Cushman describes a regional cheerleading competition for high school girls: "All through the long day in the echoing gym, the teams pranced forth and did their drills. Little girls from Catholic schools, silky spandex reflecting every prepubescent curve, ground their baby hips to sexy music in front of beaming parents and nuns."[1] Educators and parents who decry the portrayal of sex in mass media for its influence on youth support school programs which reinforce media's eroticized message.

Professional cheerleaders, who conform to prescribed images of eroticized femininity, are marketed as sexual playmates who never play. This denial mirrors the social dichotomy of Good Girl and Bad Girl. Columnist Molly Ivins has speculated about the popularity of the Dallas Cowboys Cheerleaders among religiously conservative Texans who might be expected to object to revealing costumes and suggestive dance. She quotes author Jim Schutze, who says there is no problem "as long as the presentation is locked inside a bulletproof sugar-coating of overdone, over-made-up, over-hair-sprayed, ultra-exaggerated nicey-nicey whole-someness."[2] The same sugar-coating enables beaming parents and nuns to encourage teams of little girls to grind their baby hips in the cause of school spirit.

As a stock character, the cheerleader embodies positive and negative stereotypes, reflecting contradictions and ambiguities in the cultural construction of gender roles and social ideals. The female cheerleader's expertise is easily dismissed because it serves a subordinate role. Columnist Anna Quindlen observes that while cheerleading requires "a good deal" of athletic skill, it is "really nothing more than a metaphor for traditional relationships between men and women, complete with short skirts and artificial smiles."[3]

Cheerleading also communicates externally. When Queen Elizabeth II visited Washington, D.C., in 1991, her itinerary included a demonstration of double-dutch rope jumping, basketball, and cheerleading by an inner-city Police Boys and Girls Club.[4] These activities are presented as quintessentially American inventions.

A variety of positive, negative, and ambivalent symbolism has been associated with cheerleading from the early 1900s, when it was first conveyed by mass media, to the present. Cheerleading imagery creates vivid, accessible symbols which popular culture translates into numerous, often conflicting messages.

Positive Stereotypes

Contemporary images of the cheerleader often invoke positive connotations: a young female who is physically attractive (cute), socially popular and influential—a wholesome, extroverted, enthusiastic Good Girl. These qualities mirror cultural definitions of appropriate female roles. Women are valued for youth and beauty, which convey status, and for their social role as behavioral gatekeepers and providers of emotional support. These attributes are valued across racial and socioeconomic groups. At the junior and senior high school level, the Good Girl cheerleader represents an admired elite to other students. To adults, this image continues to define youthful success and appeal. As columnist Erma Bombeck observed, "Is there a cheerleader in the Western world who answers to the name of Erma? Get real."[5] Even their names must be cute.

Being, or having been, a cheerleader is usually defined as a positive achievement. In Susan Saiter's novel *Cheerleaders Can't Afford to Be Nice* (1990), female narrator Crosby, an "A" student, a cheerleader, and a college graduate, is portrayed as the only "success" in her family.[6] This perception casts the cheerleader as a figure of prestige and privilege. In 1987 the 8th U.S. Circuit Court of Appeals struck down a Minnesota law requiring teenagers under eighteen to notify both parents or a judge forty-eight hours before having an abortion. Janet Benshoof, attorney in the appeal, said that many teenagers who were afraid to tell their parents they were pregnant also feared going to court to request an abortion: "Those least equipped for motherhood find it forced upon them. The valedictorians, the cheerleaders, go to court. It's the immature 14-year-olds that have the babies."[7] In this view, the cheerleader who gets pregnant is still a member of the social elite and is presumed to have institutional or personal resources unavailable to less fortunate girls.

A vivid example of the importance of the cheerleader as symbol made national news in 1993. When four members of the Hempstead (Texas) High School cheering squad became pregnant, one of the girls had an abortion and was allowed to return to the squad, while the girls who continued their pregnancies were ordered by the school board not to cheer, for reasons of medical liability. None of the football players, presumed to have impregnated the cheerleaders, were dismissed from the football team. The incident raised a "furor . . . [in Hempstead] about the virtues and stigmas of abortion and teenage motherhood," the responsibilities of teenage fathers, and the importance of cheerleaders as student role models.[8] National interest generated by the story reflects the significance attached to the symbol of the teen cheerleader.

The image of the cheerleader equates automatically with social success. The cheerleader is popular, never lacks a date, and is often linked socially with elite male students, such as athletes. The presumption of social success reinforces the stereotype of the cheerleader as a prize unavailable to ordinary suitors. In an episode of *Who's the Boss?*, televised in 1990, Tony recalls a "gorgeous" cheerleader in high school who everyone assumed was booked solid, until a "loser" asked her for a date and she was so "desperate," she went out with him. No one ordinarily equates the cheerleader with the wallflower.

In the pantheon of popular culture, the attractive, Good Girl cheerleader is often paired with a star male athlete. They are considered the ideal couple, particularly as head cheerleader and captain of the football or basketball team. This ideal couple image appears in numerous story lines. Sometimes it is central to the plot; sometimes it serves merely as a convention to represent a boy-girl relationship. Boy is always the athlete, a significant character, and girl is always the cheerleader, a subordinate character. The ideal couple, as used in movies such as *Tall Story* (1960) and *American Graffiti* (1973), portrays traditional roles of strong man and supportive woman. In *Tall Story*, adapted from Howard Nemerov's novel, *The Homecoming Game*, Anthony Perkins is a college basketball player and Jane Fonda is his cheerleader girlfriend.[9] His role as athlete is central to the story; her role as cheerleader is not. *American Graffiti*, set in 1962, centers around four male high school seniors, one of whom is a star athlete. The role of his head cheerleader girlfriend is secondary.[10]

In the 1980s, the ideal couple motif was expanded to permit a different emphasis. In the movie *Lucas* (1986), a high school girl who has just moved to town makes friends with a precocious, preadolescent boy who has been "accelerated" into senior high. She is encouraged to try out for cheerleading by a popular male athlete her own age, and they become the ideal couple, to the dismay of the much younger Lucas, who considers jocks and cheerleaders "superficial." The interrelationship of all three characters is important to this story, in which the cheerleader is portrayed as intelligent and thoughtful. The convention of the ideal couple focuses more on the cheerleader than the athlete and addresses stereotypes about same-age friendship.

The cheerleader personifies wholesome, extroverted leadership in the school setting. These qualities are perceived as desirable assets to carry into adult life. In 1927, cheer instructor Frank Gradler advised would-be yell leaders that "cheer-leading [is] about the finest training for future leadership in any line that a young man may follow."[11] This assumption is now applied to female cheerleaders who pursue business careers. Cheerleaders are considered natural candidates for extrovert-favored occupations such as sales and public relations. When the national Republican congressional committees hired consultant Melinda Farris to teach campaigning techniques to candidates' spouses, the *Washington Post* linked her public relations work with her background as a cheerleading instructor.[12]

The cheerleader is cast as positive and supportive, being *for* something, whether it be a team, a concept, or a cause. This image of the booster is used in any context to denote enthusiasm and advocacy. Editorial cartoonist Mike Keefe treats it humorously, depicting a group of elderly women crowded eagerly around a television set at a nursing home. While one woman leaps exuberantly, pom pons in both hands, another strikes an elderly man, who is not watching the screen, with her cane and says, "Off your can—Let's give Nolan Ryan some moral support!"[13] The cheerleader-booster is at work, encouraging aging baby boomers to identify with the then-phenomenal 46-year-old baseball pitcher. Keefe trades on the stereotype that cheerleading (and professional sport) is the purview of the young, strong, and cute.

In a 1987 essay on the fifteenth anniversary of *Ms.* magazine, Marilyn Gardner ironically applies the booster image to feminist Gloria Steinem: "At a time when the women's movement appears . . . to be at a point of transition, if not crisis, Steinem remains the last of the cheerleaders. She and she alone seems able to speak simply and confidently, as if it were 15 years ago and everybody was still in the first buoyant stage."[14] In this context, the cheerleader symbolizes the optimistic, active promoter of other people's success.

The positive stereotypic images noted above elaborate on the basic stereotype that cheerleader equals female. Beauty, social appeal, good behavior, and emotional supportiveness are values ascribed to our cultural definition of femininity.

Negative Stereotypes

For every positive cheerleader stereotype, there is a negative stereotype which is equally entrenched in popular understanding. Negative traits assigned to the female cheerleader include the following: she is dumb, conceited, and a "bimbo," a sexually promiscuous trophy for victorious males. Such qualities mirror cultural anxieties about appropriate female roles. Women who are beautiful, independent, intelligent, or sexually active threaten social expectations based on the subordinate Good Girl.

One negative metaphor is assigned to males more frequently than to females—the cheerleader as noisy, but impotent, bystander, a flak, or hired-hand mouthpiece. This image is often used in cartoons and editorials to satirize male political figures.

Because cheerleading is considered to be a feminine role, this variation is doubly insulting when applied to males.

An example is Henry Payne's editorial cartoon about George Bush's bid for the Republican nomination in 1987. A puny George Bush, dressed in cheerleading skirt and sweater, approaches a football huddle of huge Republican elephants. Bush says nervously to himself, "This is your big moment! Your chance to prove your quarterbacking skills! You're not Ronnie Reagan's cheerleader anymore! You're a lean, mean, fighting machine! . . . Golly, I think I'm getting an ulcer."[15] This stereotype casts the cheerleader as an inconsequential follower, the opposite of a quarterback, who symbolizes dynamic leadership.

Most of the negative stereotypes deal with the cheerleader's social and sexual availability. The "stuck up" cheerleader is vain and contemptuous of those outside her elite circle who can never expect to consort with her. Conversely, the cheerleader is characterized as sexually promiscuous, readily available to male achievers such as jocks, celebrities, and business tycoons. Her value as a sexual trophy is mixed. Inaccessible to many, she is a sure thing for some. Negative stereotypes about cheerleader arrogance and acquiescence reflect the tension inherent in what folklorist Gary Alan Fine calls "the dichotomy between 'the good girl' and 'the easy girl.'"[16]

The dumb cheerleader image parallels the "dumb jock" stereotype of strong body, weak mind. In cultural terms, woman is often characterized by her body rather than her mind. This stereotype is intensified for the female cheerleader in the context of sport, where athletes are assumed to have brawn instead of brain. In the comic strip "Funky Winkerbean," Westview High's cheerleaders smilingly shout, "Give us a T! Give us an E! Give us an A! Give us an M! What's that spell?" One cheerleader then turns to another and asks, "What *does* that spell?"[17] The dumb cheerleader image can be compounded with the dumb blonde image. A teenage girl wrote to columnist Lynn Minton, "I'm a blonde, and a cheerleader, and if people don't know me, they assume I'm a 'dumb blonde,' just because I cheer. And other people think—because I'm smart and in honors classes and all—that I'm some kind of geek, that I'm no fun."[18] Stereotypes in collision.

The antithesis of the cute/beautiful cheerleader is the cheerleader who is vain and conceited. Tiffany, resident gorgeous cheerleader in the comic strip "Luann," asks Luann and a friend to watch a new cheer she has just made up: "We're so hot! Lookit what we got! Watch us move! We're so smooth! We're in shape! We're—" Luann's girlfriend interrupts to ask, "Is this cheer about the team or about the cheerleaders?"[19]

Because cheerleaders are presumed to be attractive, and to be the property of the team they represent, rivals bait each other by ridiculing their opponent's cheerleaders. The following joke, submitted to the *Tonight Show* for a feature on state rivalries, is typical. Minnesotans ask, "Why do they have artificial turf on the football field at the University of Iowa?" The answer: "So the cheerleaders won't graze after the game."

The cheerleader is often equated with another stock character, the bimbo, defined by columnist Lewis Grizzard as an "air-headed young female."[20] Bimbos are of two types: benign, meaning they are sexually available, and opportunistic, meaning they are sexually available in exchange for material consideration. The former is an attractive trophy, an accessory of the successful male's lifestyle. The latter is potentially threatening to males. Benign bimbos appear in the comic strip "Sylvia." A woman describes life above the corporate "glass ceiling," which she manages to glimpse: "It was just as I'd imagined. There was an Olympic-size pool, with men in suits sitting around in lounge chairs, reading the *Wall Street Journal*. What I hadn't anticipated was the cheerleaders and the stream stocked with fish."[21] The opportunistic version appears in the comic strip "Bloom County." A little girl says, "I want to grow up and bring down dumb men in high positions! I want to be a game show hostess and earn millions! I want to star in a James Bond movie! Or a rock video! Or be a professional cheerleader! I want to grow up to be a bimbo."[22] This cheerleader is the antithesis of the supportive cheerleader helpmate image.

The stereotype of the promiscuous cheerleader is reinforced in mass media and folklore. B movies such as *The Cheerleaders* (1972), *The Pom Pom Girls* (1976), and *Cheerleaders Wild Weekend* (1985) depict cheerleaders as fantasy sexual teams which practice their sport as aggressively as the athletic teams they nominally support. They are usually portrayed in their cheerleading uniforms, even at leisure, or else they are undressed. They rarely wear "civilian" clothing. Their only dimension is sexual.

The promiscuous cheerleader is used to symbolize feminine treachery as well as feminine subservience. In a *M*A*S*H* episode originally televised in the 1970s, middle-aged Col. Henry Blake falls madly in love with winsome, twenty-year-old Ohio State cheerleader Nancy Sue Parker. While visiting camp to see Henry, Nancy meets Capt. Hawkeye Pierce and immediately makes a play for him. A shocked Hawkeye tells a friend, "Henry's Nancy just gave me a goodnight tonsillectomy you wouldn't believe." The episode resolves with Nancy's departure and Henry's reaffirmation of commitment to his wife back home. The cheerleader's betrayal is shocking to Hawkeye; Henry's betrayal is not.

Gary Alan Fine analyzed twenty-nine versions of "The Promiscuous Cheerleader" legend collected from Minnesota college students in 1977. The basic story tells of a cheerleader who voluntarily has sexual relations (usually fellatio) with every member of an athletic team. She becomes ill and is rushed to a hospital where doctors pump her stomach, removing an enormous amount of semen.[23] Most informants heard the story in high school during the early 1970s. Fine notes that this period "marked the emergence of the women's movement in the United States—a movement that threatened men in both their sexual and economic roles." He observes, "By picturing the previously submissive young woman as a victim of her own liberated sexual desires—a change from the traditional role of the sexually passive female— this adolescent male legend argues for the legitimacy of the status quo while simultaneously expressing a desire for the sexually open female."[24]

Academics also make assumptions about the sexual behavior of cheerleaders. In a 1981 study on the ideology of virginity, William H. Swatos, Jr., surveyed female college cheerleaders, considered to be a traditional role model, and female basketball players, considered as representing a nontraditional feminine role. While both groups had similar attitudes about virginity, the cheerleaders were more sexually active than the basketball players.[25]

Ambivalent Images

The most intriguing cheerleader images convey positive and negative elements simultaneously. In the comic strip "Funky Winkerbean," a middle-aged man, in his letter jacket, tells a friend, "I really can't complain . . . I was a high school football star . . . I've got a great job selling insurance . . . and I married the head cheerleader! Two outta three ain't bad!"[26] At first reading, this is a jibe at cheerleaders, but it also recognizes the cheerleader's status value to the husband and to society at large.

In a "Briefcase" cartoon, a doctor stands at a patient's bedside while two cheerleaders with pom pons strike an action pose nearby. He tells the patient, "We're going to be using a combination of chemotherapy and 'push 'em back, push 'em back, waaay back.'"[27] This image can be read as a frivolous extension of the cheerleader-booster role, but it also acknowledges the value of positive thinking in medical recovery and the cheerleader's symbolic representation of optimistic support.

A recent movie, *Buffy, the Vampire Slayer* (1992), features "an airheaded high-school cheerleader who . . . has been chosen by history to defend her schoolmates from the deadly threat of blood-sucking vampires."[28] Female action heroes are relatively scarce. Some, like Wonder Woman, have super powers, or the assistance of super androids, like Linda Hamilton's character in the *Terminator* movies. Female heroes like Buffy, and Sigourney Weaver in the *Alien* series, are ordinary citizens who must use their own resources. To give a blonde airhead heroic responsibility is to recognize the acceptance of women in a variety of nontraditional occupational roles. At the same time, Buffy can be read as a spoof of feminine competence, a joke to be lightly dismissed.

High culture has also employed ambivalent elements in the cheerleader image. For an exhibit titled "The Body Electric" at the Corcoran Gallery of Art, sculptor Zizi Raymond made a crucifix of "a perky statuette from a cheerleading trophy." As critic Hank Burchard notes, "the image fixes itself in the mind and won't stop resonating."[29]

Symbolic Uses and Perceptions

Cheerleading functions in a variety of social and commercial contexts. It contributes to civic identity via sports ritual and ceremony. Cheerleading imagery is used by adults to create role models and cautionary tales for youth. It is used in advertising and merchandising, and it serves as a vehicle for adult ambition and fantasy.

The ritualistic value of cheerleading to a school was described by Charles Glicksberg in 1945:

> The school colors, the bright uniforms of the band led
> by the resplendent major domo, the strutting twirlers
> performing before the grandstand, the school cheers led
> by the acrobatic cheer leaders, the school song . . . all
> these make up much of the life of the school and keep
> up its morale.[30]

This element of pageantry is so important that deaf high school and college students field cheerleading squads who root at games and conduct pep rallies in sign language.[31]

The significance of local sports to community identity, particularly in rural areas, is also well established. Movies such as *Hoosiers* (1987) illustrate the intensity of civic involvement with school sports. When the high school in Hedrich, Iowa, population 847, fielded girls' and boys' basketball teams in 1983, "so many of the school's 23 girls preferred playing hoops to eliciting rah-rahs," that none went out for cheerleading.[32] The community, determined to have a cheering squad, recruited six grandmothers to lead cheers for the season. The Granny Squad agreed to continue another year if the high school girls still did not want to cheer.

In Mountainair, New Mexico, the rituals of school pageantry are so important that high school cheerleaders and football players march in the band at halftime for home games. Because there is no time to change into band uniforms, the cheerleaders and ball players perform in their respective uniforms. The boys march in their cleats but remove their helmets.[33] In both cases, the communities and schools use alternative ways to maintain rituals which are important to them.

Adults use images of cheerleaders and athletes as role models to teach youth moral lessons and encourage desired behavior. The Children's Defense Fund, active in programs to prevent teen pregnancy, uses posters which trade on the prestige of cheerleaders and athletes. A poster directed to girls shows a smiling ten-girl cheering squad. It reads, "Get pregnant and clothes won't be the only thing you can't get into." A companion poster for boys shows a serious young male holding an infant. Its message: "An extra seven pounds could keep you off the football team."[34]

Authors of juvenile literature use cheerleading to attract young readers and convey social and ethical lessons. In *Three Cheers for Polly* (1967), a girl fails to become captain of the cheering squad until she learns to take responsibility. *Gimme an H, Gimme an E, Gimme an L, Gimme a P* (1980) is the story of a gifted high school boy who befriends a popular, intelligent, but suicidal girl cheerleader. *The Cheerleader* (1985) treats flexibility in gender roles as ninth-grade boys form a cheerleading squad for a girls' sports team. In *Cheating* (1985), high school cheerleaders deal with ethical issues when they suspect star basketball players of throwing games. *Have a Heart, Cupid Delaney!* (1986) addresses exclusion and stereotyping when a football star and a head cheerleader fall in love with two unpopular students due to mistakes made by a Cupid-in-training.[35]

Despite such well-intentioned versions, some students rebel at the cheerleader-jock role models. At Harvard University in 1990, students formed the Society of Nerds and Geeks, a coeducational group to combat anti-intellectualism among undergraduates. A Society spokesman told the *Chronicle of Higher Education*, "At Harvard nerds are ostracized while jocks are idolized. . . . We're never going to be able to keep up with the East Asian countries if our society keeps making the captain of the football team and the head cheerleader our heroes."[36]

The image of the cheerleader as an epitome of youthful success is offset by images of decline in adult life. News stories about female criminals and crime victims invariably note any cheerleading in the woman's background. In the first instance, the assumption of a good girl gone bad adds color; in the second, there is added fascination that someone once idolized has been victimized. Such reports serve as cautionary tales that the mighty can fall or, at least, struggle. This is a theme in Michael Hoffman's film, *Promised Land* (1987), which traces the disappointments and compromises faced by a small-town high school basketball star and his cheerleader girlfriend after they graduate and go separate ways.[37]

As a pervasive theme in popular culture, cheerleading is used in advertising and merchandising to target children, teens, and adults. Cheerleading is used to market toys, particularly dolls, to girls, just as it markets fantasy to adult males. The Handicraft All American Cheerleader Set, containing a baton, two pom pons, and a megaphone, available at Wal-Mart for $8.68, pictures a young, blonde girl on the package. Mattel's Barbie, of course, has appeared as a cheerleader, along with her satellite, Courtney, and their competition doll, Hasbro's Maxie.[38] Maxie's outfit includes a letter jacket, signifying that she is part of an ideal couple. Cheerleader Maxie has also been featured in television commercials during children's programs. The upscale Madame Alexander line of dolls includes a serious-faced cheerleader, and the currently popular Treasure Trolls include a barefoot Troll cheerleader.[39]

The School Colors Sally Rally doll, which can be customized by race and hair color and costumed in any two specified school colors, is available by mail order. This clever marketing device is aimed at adults as "a doll your cheerleader will cherish long after her school days are over."[40]

Advertisers targeting mass magazines for the teenage market use the cheerleader image to sell cosmetics and grooming aids to adolescent girls. 'Teen magazine touts Aziza cosmetics for the game: "Power Pencil in Plum plus Burgundy Black Mascara with Sealer team up for the eyes. And lips get ready to cheer with Natural Lustre Lip Gloss."[41] Articles naming advertisers' products feature cheerleaders, who, by definition, need no such help; they are aimed at girls who hope to emulate the acknowledged beauties.

Seventeen uses the "makeover" device common in women's magazines to show members of a high school squad before and after new haircuts and professional makeup jobs.[42] Remedial advice for the already beautiful reinforces unrealistic cultural expectations of feminine beauty aimed at schoolgirls.

Cheerleading targets the adult market indirectly, selling itself to parents who purchase the image for their children. Commercially produced children's Halloween costumes have become increasingly elaborate in recent years. Generic drum major and cheerleader costumes, for boys and girls respectively, are offered in sizes 6 to 10, complete with gold braid and pom pons.[43] Sports boutiques and colleges sell children's cheerleading outfits which feature specific team colors and logos. They are designed for girls. Products for boys tend to replicate players' uniforms or warmup suits.[44]

Since the popular perception of cheerleading is loaded with emotional implications, it presents vivid opportunities to depict scandal and sensation. In the 1990s, two incidents put cheerleading in the national headlines of mainstream and tabloid news, talk shows, and made-for-television movies. The Transvestite Cheerleader and the Cheerleader Hit Mom captured mass media attention because their sensational stories challenged cultural beliefs about gender, competition, childhood, and parenthood.

In 1990, Charles Daugherty, a twenty-six-year-old, five-foot, eight-inch, 160-pound male, enrolled as a junior at a Colorado Springs, Colorado, high school, posing as a girl. Using the name Cheyen Weatherly, he joined the school choir, became a cheerleader (without a formal tryout), and performed in uniform at a pep rally. His ruse was discovered after eight days and he was arrested and charged with forgery of school transcripts and criminal impersonation. He was sentenced in 1991 to two years of probation with mandatory counseling. The story was carried by The Associated Press and Scripps Howard News Service.

Daugherty appeared on the Sally Jessy Raphael show and in *Esquire* magazine.[45]

Daugherty violated both gender and age taboos by successfully posing as a sixteen-year-old girl. The fact that he fooled adolescents, who are quick to judge each other's appearance, as well as school officials, calls into question assumptions about conventions such as age grouping and gender identification. For him to be accepted as a female cheerleader challenges perceptions of femininity and physical attractiveness in the competitive context of adolescent social hierarchies. This incident pales, however, in comparison with the blockbuster Cheerleader Hit Mom story.

In 1991, Wanda Webb Holloway, of Channelview (!), Texas, was arrested and charged with solicitation of capital murder in a plot to hire a hit man to kill the mother of a thirteen-year-old girl who was competing with Holloway's daughter to join the school cheerleading squad. Holloway was convicted and sentenced to fifteen years in prison plus a $10,000 fine, but the conviction was overturned in 1992 because one of the jurors was discovered to be a felon. In October 1994, the First District of Texas Court of Appeals upheld the lower court's decision to throw out Holloway's conviction. At present, a retrial is pending.[46]

The Cheerleader Hit Mom—or Pom Pom Mom—saga hit newspapers, tabloids, *People Weekly,* and *Tonight Show* monologues, and has inspired two television movies, *Willing To Kill: The Texas Cheerleader Story* and *The Positively True Adventures of the Alleged Texas Cheerleader-Murdering Mom,* to date. Jokes abounded: "What's the difference between a pit bull and a cheerleader's mother?" Answer: "Lipstick." Johnny Carson cheered, "Gimme a G, gimme a U, gimme an N" and Jay Leno said that if Saddam Hussein acted up again, "Just tell that woman in Texas his daughter is going out for cheerleading."

This "yummily grotesque true story" is so fascinating that a *Washington Post* reviewer wondered how it got turned into "such a clumsy, unconvincing and essentially drab TV movie."[47] The truth of the Hit Mom story is too awful to embellish. It defies efforts to exaggerate either the terrible intensity or the pitiful triviality of the situation. The incident contradicts basic cultural ideology about the innocence of schoolgirl pursuits, the healthy, character-building nature of competitive school activities, notions of fair play, that winning isn't everything, and that failure teaches useful lessons. Holloway, described as the ultimate stage mother, violates ideology about "normal" maternal protectiveness and the vicarious rewards of parenting. In pathological efforts on her daughter's behalf, Holloway obliterated her child's autonomy, not to mention that of the intended victims, and substituted her own inappropriate ambition. To lose sight of reality is a frightening prospect. To lose all perspective in pursuit of a trivial cause is tragic. In making junior high popularity and competition, symbolized by cheerleading, a matter of life and death, Holloway presents a compelling irony for public contemplation.

What Cheerleading Means to Cheerleaders

Cheerleading has many meanings to observers of popular culture. What does it mean to those who participate directly? Does the experience of cheerleading reflect the cultural values ascribed to it?

In a 1983 survey of high school seniors in Mesa, Arizona, 37 percent indicated "the school activity that helped them most was athletics and cheerleading."[48] These students confirm the position of educators who stress the positive social benefits of extracurricular activities.

For some, the status signified by getting selected as cheerleader is more important than cheering itself. Sportswriter Pat Ryan reported that, for university cheerleaders at Ole Miss in the 1960s, "the sweat is largely devoted to attaining the position, not performing in it." After elaborate campaigning and electioneering, successful candidates "have been known to semiretire. Some have not shown up at bowl games until halftime."[49]

To at least one high school cheerleader, glamour was tempered by physical realities. Mary-Ellen Banashek wrote in *Mademoiselle*:

> October, 1968, and I'm sitting in a steady drizzle, shouting "You can do it if you try, V-I-C-T-O-R-Y!" With less than four minutes left in the game, my team is trailing 55–0. Mud is splattered all over my legs, my crepe paper pom-poms are beginning to run and . . . I'm finding out it's tough to be a status symbol.[50]

Anecdotes by former cheerleaders reveal a variety of perspectives on the experience: "I'm wondering if [cheering] helped me to be positive in my approach to life now. I think it did!"—Annette Carlson, junior and senior high cheerleader, Blencoe, Iowa, 1938–42.[51] "It is always something to remember and an honor to have been allowed to represent your school."—Arlene Adcock, junior, senior high, and college cheerleader, Blencoe and Sioux City, Iowa, 1939–43.[52] "Being a cheerleader helped me overcome extreme shyness. . . . [As an adult], I was happy to relate to my children when they participated in sports."—Huldah McQuillen, high school cheerleader, Fairfax, Virginia, 1943–44.[53] "It was the only form of sport there was for girls at that time. . . . We were all very athletic and driven to be good athletes as well as good cheerleaders."—Nancy Fearheiley, junior varsity and varsity cheerleader, Mt. Carmel, Illinois, 1966–70.[54]

At Plainfield (Indiana) Community Middle School, known for having a "no-cut" policy in all extracurricular activities, one of its seventy-three cheerleaders said, "I'm going to high school next year, and I know I won't make the cheerleading squad there. I know there are a lot of girls who are better at it than I am. But at least I got to have the experience. And that's something I can remember all my life."[55] For such students, the act of participating is important; for the Ole Miss cheerleaders, in contrast, what mattered was the cachet of an exclusionary selection process.

That individuals include their cheerleading background in public statements such as engagement notices and obituaries attests to its significance for them. Cheerleading is listed as an achievement along with college attendance, employment history, and volunteer work.[56]

Popular culture portrays the cheerleader as a celebrity. Admired and envied, or not, cheerleaders are well known within the context of their school or community. It is also common to link national celebrities and cheerleading in interviews and profiles of their personal background. For a 1974 story in *Esquire* magazine, Nancy Collins interviewed women celebrities who had been cheerleaders. Their comments provide additional perspectives on what cheerleading means to those who have done it:

> Fashion designer Betsey Johnson, high school and college cheerleader at Syracuse University: "I was really serious about it and worked very hard to be good. . . . You are a show girl, a no-touch exhibitionist. Actually, it's the same trip I have now—glamour, responsibility, power. Not only that, I'm still making little uniforms."

Actress Ann-Margret, cheerleader at New Trier (Illinois) High School: "Believe me, I worked as hard as any of the football players."

Actress Pat Morrow, cheerleader for all-girl Providence High School, Burbank, California: "Girls weren't supposed to be aggressive, but being a cheerleader gave you license to be loud and extroverted. And the license to make decisions, even though you were locked into a stereotype."

Television news writer Carol Ross, cheerleader at Fort Hunt (Virginia) High School: "When I stood in front of the stands leading cheers, I felt I had the world in my hands. I was a celebrity. I knew what real power was."[57]

Actor Patrick Duffy, a high school cheerleader in the 1960s, reported a different motivation. After trying football, Duffy became a cheerleader "to be with the best-looking women in the school."[58]

Other famous Americans who knew early celebrity as cheerleaders include: Kirstie Alley; Kim Basinger; Barbi Benton; Katie Couric, Yorktown H.S., Arlington, Virginia; Faye Dunaway; Dwight D. Eisenhower, U.S. Military Academy; Donna Fargo; Sally Field, Birmingham H.S., Van Nuys, California; Phyllis George; Eydie Gorme, William Taft H.S., Bronx, New York; Ben Hecht, Racine (Washington) H.S.; Kay Bailey Hutchison, La Marque (Texas) H.S. and University of Texas.

Also, Cheryl Ladd, Huron (South Dakota) H.S.; Vicki Lawrence; Jack Lemmon, Phillips Academy, Andover, Massachusetts; Jerry Lewis, Irvington (New Jersey) H.S.; Susan Lucci, Garden City (New York) H.S.; Shirley MacLaine, Washington-Lee H.S., Arlington, Virginia; Madonna, Adams H.S., Rochester, Michigan; Steve Martin, Garden Grove (California) H.S.; Michael Milken, Birmingham H.S., Van Nuys, California; Queen Noor, the former Lisa Halaby, Princeton (member of Princeton's first coeducational class and its first coeducational cheering squad); Mary Kay Place; Cole Porter, Yale; Ronald Reagan, Eureka College; John Reed, Harvard; Susan Sarandon; Patty Hearst Shaw, Sacred Heart Prep School, Menlo Park, California; Cybill Shepherd; Dinah Shore, Hume-Fogg H.S., Nashville, Tennessee; Carly Simon, Riverdale Girls' School, Bronx, New York; Pamela South, Salmon (Idaho) H.S.; Sissy Spacek; Meryl Streep,

Bernardsville (New Jersey) H.S.; Sally Struthers, U.S. Grant H.S., Portland, Oregon; Loretta Swit; Cheryl Tiegs; Lily Tomlin, Cass Technical H.S., Detroit, Michigan; Raquel Welch, La Jolla (California) H.S.; and Vanna White, North Myrtle Beach (South Carolina) H.S.[59]

On the other hand, some tried and failed. A few who have described their unsuccessful tryouts (and vivid disappointment) include: Sandy Duncan, Lauren Hutton, Diane Keaton, Valerie Perrine, and Dory Previn.[60] Two women, however, credit their failure to become cheerleaders as the stimulus that led to their adult careers. Television journalist Jane Pauley said: "I didn't make varsity cheerleader. At the age of 14, I felt my life was over. I ended up joining the speech team instead. . . . My event was Girls' Extemporaneous Speaking. They would give you a topic, and a half-hour later you made a seven-minute speech on it. . . . I can't imagine better preparation for what I do today."[61] Actress Swoosie Kurtz, who performs in *The Positively True Adventures of the Alleged Texas Cheerleader-Murdering Mom*, recalled her own cheerleader tryout: "I was going gung-ho and then literally tripped. . . . I fell flat on my face. . . . I failed miserably and went immediately into drama and black tights and never went in the sun again."[62]

"Cheerleader Wish," as Erma Bombeck calls it, affects thousands of girls because being a cheerleader personifies most of the cultural expectations which have defined successful femininity since the 1920s: beauty and popularity, which confer prestige upon girls and their male associates, and the emotionally supportive, but always subordinate, role women are expected to serve, even as public entertainers. The cachet of being a cheerleader has fluctuated in recent decades. As Barbara Roessner notes, "Cheerleading has always been a finely tuned barometer of social change."[63] She recalls that in the late 1950s, "being a cheerleader was everything a girl dreamed of" and her older sister was "devastated" when her parents refused to let her try out. By the time Roessner entered high school in the late 1960s, she viewed cheerleaders as "shallow, stupid, blind participants in a particularly vile form of exploitation." Her parents "begged" her to try out, "to demonstrate . . . interest in anything remotely 'wholesome.'"[64] By the 1970s, Title IX gave girls additional opportunities to compete in athletics. They were no longer restricted to cheerleading or drill teams. In 1975, physical education teacher Christine Sears told the *New York Times* that "more and more girls have their choice of varsity activities—of playing the game or cheering the plays."[65] She urged girls to "have an appreciation for what someone else chooses to do." With the advent of competitive cheering, girls have additional reasons to participate.

Gender Roles

Most of the images discussed in this chapter portray the cheerleader as female. The preponderance of feminine references reflects both fact and fallacy. In terms of numbers of participants, cheerleading has been a predominantly feminine activity since the 1950s. Males, however, have always served as cheerleaders. Historic images of cheering provide evidence that it has been coeducational, to varying degrees, since the 1920s. The overriding contemporary perception that cheerleader equals girl is reinforced by popular culture which defines it strictly in feminized terms.

Cultural lag occurs because perceptions change more slowly than events. Cheerleading is particularly entrenched as a feminine activity because it complements sports, an activity perceived as masculine. Like cheerleading, sports is characterized as the purview of one gender, even though both women and men participate.

Images of cheerleading reflect societal anxiety about current gender roles, reinforcing the status quo, but occasionally offering a glimpse of change in progress. Two cartoons exemplify ambivalent scenarios about contemporary gender roles. Cartoonists Bunny Hoest and John Reiner picture two career women on their way home from work. One looks at her front door where her husband, holding pom pons, leaps joyfully in the air. She says to her fellow commuter, "Steve has been very supportive about my job."[66] This cartoon pokes fun at the idea of switching gender-defined provider and homemaker roles, but it does allow for the possibility.

In the comic strip "For Better or For Worse," a squad of high school girls practices cheering, "Smash 'em! Trash 'em! Rush 'em! Crush 'em! For the thrill, we're gonna KILL, Ya better call your next of kin! Come on, Red Hawks, WIN, WIN, WIN!" Watching from the bleachers, one teenage boy says to another, "So much for the weaker sex!"[67] The girls show a zeal for combat which females are not supposed to exhibit, but it is contained in an appropriately feminine context, supporting male warriors.

Contemporary images in mass culture continue to portray cheerleading primarily in conventionally feminine terms. In actuality, increased opportunities in women's sports and cheering have created a dilemma for girls similar to the "double day" faced by women who are employed. They are permitted to pursue non-traditional challenges, as long as they also maintain traditionally assigned roles. In 1978, the *Denver Post* profiled four girls from rural Ridgway (Colorado) High School who were members of the school's undefeated basketball team and also on the cheerleading squad supporting the boys' junior varsity and varsity basketball teams. Taking both uniforms with them on game nights, the girls would play their game and then cheer for both boys' games. When asked which she enjoyed more, one girl responded, "Playing, I guess. There's more personal rewards."[68]

A 1984 feature on the Greenup County (Kentucky) High School cheering squad noted the girls had won four national cheer championships. When the school's football coach was asked to comment, he responded that "School spirit is essential. . . . Our cheerleaders have given our student athletes the support we need to have a very successful school athletic program."[69] Girls may cheer competitively at the national level, but that achievement is secondary to their role as helpmates to the local boys' team. The cheerleader icon, now established in feminine terms, has been slow to reflect the changing content of contemporary cheerleading. The ambiguities and contradictions in cheerleading imagery reflect conflicting cultural values about gender roles in the wider social arena.

6

Thinking About Cheerleading:
Reiteration and Reinterpretation

An examination of cheerleading reveals the contrast between symbolism and reality in the development of a unique expression of American culture. In reality, cheerleading is pervasive in community, school, and professional sports. Symbolically, it permeates mass media and popular culture. Events and factors which shaped cheerleading have been described in an effort to analyze its significance as a vivid cultural icon of success, sport, and sexuality. As an icon, cheerleading both reflects and reinforces social norms and values. Over time, the reality and the mythology have become increasingly complex. It is possible to trace variations in congruence and dissonance between the reality of cheerleading and the symbolism attached to it.

Cheerleading has gone through many structural and stylistic changes since it was invented by male college students for their own amusement in the late 1800s. Cultural perceptions of cheerleading have also changed, particularly as it became a feminized activity. The tension between positive and negative images of cheerleading in contemporary culture reflects contradictions and complexities in socially constructed gender roles. The subjective characterization of cheerleading is closely bound to traditionally defined gender behavior. An emerging trend toward flexibility in gender roles is becoming evident in contemporary cheerleading, but it is overshadowed by the symbolic portrayal of cheerleading in feminized terms.

When cheering spread to public secondary schools in the 1900s, educators redefined it to teach and to reinforce desired student behavior. During the 1950s, entrepreneurs created an industry to service and supply cheerleading. In the process, they invented and promoted cheering as a competitive event. Professional sport organizations appropriated one form of cheerleading in the 1970s for mass marketing and entertainment. Each of these redefinitions affected cultural assumptions about cheerleading.

The basic function of cheerleading, to provide emotional support to an athletic team during competition, has endured for a century, but additional functions have been added. Cheerleaders are expected to serve as student leaders and to foster school morale beyond the playing field. In many communities they contribute to civic identity which is closely tied to school athletics. School and college cheerleaders provide entertainment for audiences in addition to supporting athletic teams on the field. Spirit groups such as drill teams and mascots have evolved from cheerleading to increase the variety of pageantry and spectacle in sports events. Cheerleading has become a designated activity in suburban and inner-city youth programs. As an emerging sport, competitive cheerleading now provides an athletic outlet as well as a focus for school and community identity.

The demographic profile of cheerleaders has changed considerably since the first yell leader stepped out of the crowd in the rarified atmosphere of nineteenth-century collegiate life. When cheering reached the public schools, younger students, both male and female, began to participate, first at the secondary level, then in junior high and elementary grades. By the 1950s, middle- and working-class children cheerleading in public and private schools outnumbered those in the college elite. With the civil rights movement of the 1960s, racial representation in cheerleading and other extracurricular activities became an issue in many schools and colleges.

As cheerleading changed and diversified, different images of the cheerleader proliferated in American culture. The first cheerleaders, privileged college men, were seen as heroic figures, part of the masculine world of sport and competition. Fellow warriors with players on the field, these cheerleaders exemplified leadership and athleticism. Cheerleading in this era was viewed as a prestigious, masculine activity. At this point in early cheerleading, there was congruence between image and reality. Male cheerleaders fulfilled a masculine role.

When cheerleading reached into the coeducational public schools, it was accessible to many more students. As female students joined the ranks on the sidelines, the role of the cheerleader came to be viewed in feminized terms, as supportive and entertaining, rather than heroic. Since women were not considered fellow warrior-athletes, their role as cheerleaders was diminished to a subordinate, ornamental status—a status often assigned to women in general. This image of cheerleading has dominated popular perception from the 1950s to the present. It is reinforced by the numeric predominance of females in scholastic, collegiate, and professional cheerleading. While males have continued to lead cheers and coeducational squads have existed since the 1920s, cheerleading has been feminized in fact as well as perception. Mass media emphasis on images such as erotically packaged professional cheerleaders and fanatical "hit moms" reinforces perceptions that cheerleading is a feminine realm. At present, there is both congruence and dissonance between the reality of cheerleading and the way it is portrayed in popular culture.

The image of cheerleading as a feminine role is so entrenched in popular understanding that scholarly analysts tend to emphasize it and overlook the subtleties in gender role participation which contemporary cheering actually provides. George Kurman describes his 1986 article, "What Does Girls' Cheerleading Communicate?," as "a contribution to a semiotic approach to the composite spectacle of the American school basketball or football game."[1] Kurman states that his essay "avoids the complications introduced by co-educational cheerleading." He then describes cheerleading as an expression and reinforcement of traditional female roles. Discussion of male cheerleaders, who are also active in the spectacle of school and college sports, is omitted because it would undermine his argument that cheering represents a wholly feminine activity.

In his book *Sport in Society: Issues and Controversies*, published in 1990, Jay Coakley asks if cheerleaders are

> the living dinosaurs of American sport. . . . In the midst
> of our growing awareness about the unfairness and
> destructiveness of traditional definitions of masculinity
> and femininity, cheerleaders stand out as symbols of the
> past . . . on the sidelines serving as attractive showpieces
> for the teams they represent.[2]

Coakley's discussion ignores the existence of male cheerleaders as well as the emergence of increasingly athletic and competitive forms of cheerleading. Both factors merit examination because they challenge "traditional definitions of masculinity and femininity" in cheering. Boys do cheer and girls do compete.

One analyst who does consider a variety of gender issues in cheerleading concludes that it preserves conventional gender roles. In her essay "Male Cheerleaders and the Naturalization of Gender," Laurel Davis describes petite, attractive female cheerleaders who provide support for male athletes and voyeuristic interest for a male audience—an accepted female role. She characterizes male cheerleaders as contributing strength in stunts which "present" female cheerleaders to the crowd—physical prowess and control as an accepted male role. Davis sees a sexual division of labor in cheerleading which "reinforces traditional gender beliefs, including notions of men's natural physical superiority."[3] Her discussion ignores the fact that many female squads perform the same demanding stunts without male assistance and that male cheerleaders are also on display to the crowd. Each of these scholars omits discussion of actual nontraditional gender roles in order to argue that cheerleading is still traditionally feminine or masculine.

Today, both school and college cheerleading provide some flexibility in gender role participation, although these changes are limited in number and degree. Professional cheerleading, in contrast, is still rigidly feminized. Male and female cheerleaders now perform in support of female athletic teams. Changes in the content of cheering permit males and females to fulfill roles previously defined as feminine and masculine, respectively. Since supportive and entertainment aspects of cheerleading remain important, males participate in that context as well as the purely athletic. The increased athleticism of cheerleading means that females participate as athletes, not just as ornaments. Along with athleticism, the trend toward competitive cheerleading has helped to establish cheerleading as a sport. This designation creates another avenue for females to compete as athletes. The presence of mixed-sex squads in competition showcases athletic skills and cooperation among females and males alike.

In cheerleading today, both females and males function in contexts previously restricted to the opposite gender. While change is happening, it is subtle. To the observer, cheerleading still appears to be a feminine activity. The majority of cheerleaders are female and they are still seen most often on the sidelines. In this sense, there is congruence between image and reality. It is too early for popular opinion to reflect the flexibility of gender roles which is gradually occurring in school and college cheerleading. Cheering was first established as a masculine role. It took some fifty years to be reestablished, in reality and symbolically, as a feminine activity. Cultural perceptions might eventually recognize the fluidity and variety of gender roles which is beginning to emerge in contemporary cheering, but at present this reality is overwhelmed by the image of feminized cheerleading.

Cheerleading is a pervasive, enduring icon that both reflects and reinforces American values and institutions. Beyond its representation of gender roles, cheerleading personifies fundamental themes of American mythology such as rugged individualism which extends to celebrity or stardom, democratic cooperation idealized as fair play or teamwork, and a competitive work ethic which culminates in victory, success, or financial profit. Cheerleading portrays aspects of militarism with its stress on disciplined, unified performance in the ritualized combat of organized sport. It reflects corporate capitalism and entrepreneurial interests in advertising and merchandising. It objectifies social anxieties about failure and success. The iconographic significance of cheerleading functions in many contexts, serves many different agendas, and appeals to a broad social and demographic spectrum. The reality of cheerleading as an American invention is greatly magnified by its symbolic power in American culture.

Notes

Introduction

1. Charles Thomas Hatton and Robert W. Hatton, "The Sideline Show," *Journal of the National Association for Women Deans, Administrators, and Counselors* 42 (Fall 1978), 23.

2. *The Oxford English Dictionary,* 2nd ed., vol. 3 (Oxford: Clarendon Press, 1989), 75.

3. Joseph Nathan Kane, *Facts About the Presidents,* 5th ed. (New York: H.W. Wilson, 1989), 193.

4. "The Broadening Curriculum," *New York Times,* 25 Jan. 1924, 16.

5. Nancy Collins, "Girls of Autumn: For Ex-cheerleaders, the Pompoms Sag But Life Goes On," *Esquire* 82 (Oct. 1974), 221.

6. John Goodger, "Ritual Solidarity and Sport," *Acta Sociologica (Norway)* 29, no. 3 (1986), 222.

7. *Webster's Ninth New Collegiate Dictionary* (Springfield, MA: Merriam-Webster, 1989), 230.

8. Robert A. Palmatier and Harold L. Ray, *Sports Talk: A Dictionary of Sports Metaphors* (New York: Greenwood Press, 1989), 26.

9. *Oxford English Dictionary,* vol. 12, 89.

10. Quoted in Ellen K. Coughlin, "Scholars in the Humanities Are Disheartened by the Course of Debate Over Their Disciplines," *Chronicle of Higher Education,* 13 Sept. 1989, A14.

1. Collegiate and Scholastic Beginnings

1. Helen Lefkowitz Horowitz, *Campus Life: Undergraduate Cultures from the End of the Eighteenth Century to the Present* (New York: Knopf, 1987), xi.

2. Gregory S. Sojka, "Evolution of the Student-Athlete in America," *Journal of Popular Culture* 16 (Spring 1983), 55.

3. Ibid.

4. Horowitz, *Campus Life,* 39.

5. Grace W. Stark, "Fun in College," *Peabody Journal of Education* 21 (Mar. 1944), 269-74.

6. Hatton and Hatton, "The Sideline Show," 24.

7. Arturo F. Gonzales, Jr., "The First College Cheer," *American Mercury* 83 (Nov. 1956), 101.

8. Ibid., 103.

9. Ralph D. Paine, "The Spirit of School and College Sport in English and American Football," *Century* 71 (Nov. 1905), 107-12.

10. Ibid., 111.

11. Horowitz, *Campus Life*, 50; Paine, "The Spirit of School and College Sport," 99.

12. Hatton and Hatton, "The Sideline Show," 24.

13. Newt Loken and Otis Dypwick, *Cheerleading & Marching Bands* (New York: Ronald Press, 1945), xi.

14. Gonzales, "The First College Cheer," 103.

15. "Organized Cheering," *The Nation* 92 (5 Jan. 1911), 5-6,

16. Horowitz, *Campus Life*, 53-54.

17. Ibid.

18. William T. Foster, "Athletics by Proxy," *School and Society* 1 (22 May 1915), 738.

19. W.H. Cowley, "Explaining the Rah Rah Boy," *New Republic* 46 (14 Apr. 1926), 243.

20. "November Yells That Win Games," *Literary Digest* 83 (8 Nov. 1924), 36; Frank A. Gradler, *Psychology and Technique of Cheer-leading: A Handbook for Cheer-leaders* (Menomonie, WI: Menomonie Athletic Book Supply, 1927), 8.

21. Paula S. Fass, *The Damned and the Beautiful: American Youth in the 1920's* (Oxford: Oxford University Press, 1979), 238.

22. "November Yells," 34; George M. York and H.H. Clark, *Just Yells: A Guide for Cheer Leaders* (Syracuse, NY: Willis N. Bugbee, 1927), 31.

23. York, *Just Yells*, Foreword.

24. Hatton and Hatton, "The Sideline Show," 27.

25. Randy Neil, *The Encyclopedia of Cheerleading*, 3rd ed. (Shawnee Mission, KS: International Cheerleading Foundation, 1975), 75.

26. Ibid.; "Sis, Boom, Ah! Short History of the Art of Cheering," *Scholastic* 32 (12 Mar. 1938), 29.

27. Loken, *Cheerleading and Marching Bands*, 44.

28. "The Yell-leader: An American Functionary," *Times* (London) *Educational Supplement* 755 (19 Oct. 1929), 456.

29. *Mirage* (San Antonio: Trinity University, 1923), 78; (1925), 124; (1929), 122; (1936), 60; (1938), 55; (1939), 90.

30. "All-America," *Time* 34 (11 Dec. 1939), 42.

31. Ibid.

32. Barbara M. Solomon, *In the Company of Educated Women: A History of Women and Higher Education in America* (New Haven: Yale University Press, 1985), 17.

33. Horowitz, *Campus Life*, 202.

34. Ibid., 208.

35. Fass, *The Damned,* 145.

36. Ibid., 144-45.

37. John D'Emilio and Estelle Freedman, *Intimate Matters: A History of Sexuality in America* (New York: Harper & Row, 1988), 233.

38. York, *Just Yells,* passim; Gradler, *Psychology and Technique of Cheer-leading,* passim.

39. Loken and Dypwick, *Cheerleading & Marching Bands;* Bruce A. Turvold, *The Art of Cheerleading* (Minneapolis: Northwestern Press, 1948).

40. "Women's Lib Rah! Rah!" *New York Times,* 19 Jan. 1975, 103.

41. Bruce Newman, "Eight Beauties and a Beat," *Sports Illustrated* 54 (16 Mar. 1981), 33.

42. "Spry Gals' Giant Leap," *Life* 47 (2 Nov. 1959), 59-60.

43. Fass, *The Damned,* 211.

44. Benjamin G. Rader, *American Sports: From the Age of Folk Games to the Age of Spectators* (Englewood Cliffs: Prentice-Hall, 1983), 161-62.

45. Quoted in Rader, *American Sports,* 162.

46. Ibid., 161.

47. Ibid.

48. Ethel Percy Andrus, "School Spirit," *National Education Association Proceedings and Addresses* (1917), 529-30.

49. Gertrude W. Morrison, *The Girls of Central High at Basketball, or, The Great Gymnasium Mystery* (Akron, OH: Saalfield Publishing, 1914), 46.

50. "November Yells," 38.

51. Ibid., 36.

52. Franklin M. Reck, "All Aboard the Pep Special!" *World Review* 7 (15 Oct. 1928), 74.

53. Janet Singer, *Cheer Leader* (Chicago: Goldsmith Publishing, 1934), 13.

54. John J. Gach, "The Case For and Against Girl Cheerleaders," *School Activities* 9 (Mar. 1938), 301-02.

55. "They Don't Boo; Do You? Pepnocrats of Connersville, Ind. High School," *Scholastic* 31 (13 Nov. 1937), 31.

56. Ibid.

57. "High-school Cheerleaders: Agile Trio at Whiting, Ind. Specialize in Rhythm-nastics," *Life* 11 (10 Nov. 1941), 58.

58. Ibid., 60.

59. Lawrence M. Brings, *School Yells: Suggestions for Cheerleaders* (Minneapolis: Northwestern Press, 1944), 9.

60. Loken and Dypwick, *Cheerleading & Marching Bands,* xii.

61. Virginia Nilles, "Cheerleading," *New York State Education* 42 (Mar. 1955), 392-93.

62. Ibid.

63. Mia Fonssagrives, "Speaking of Pictures," *Life* 37 (25 Oct. 1954), 11.

64. Harold Hainfeld, "Cheerleading in Grade and Junior High," *School Activities* 30 (Dec. 1958), 116-17.

65. Newt Loken, *Cheerleading,* 2nd ed. (Malabar, FL: Krieger, 1983 reprint of 1961 ed.), 5.

66. Ibid., 10.

67. Marylou Humphrey and Ron Humphrey, *Cheerleading and Song Leading* (Rutland: Charles E. Tuttle, 1970), 11.

68. Ibid., 131.

69. Neil, *Encyclopedia of Cheerleading*, 234.

70. Orlino Castro, *RPH-30: A Pom-pon Team* (Hawaiian Gardens, CA: J. Witherspoon Publications, 1975), 8.

71. Ibid., 12.

72. Neil, *Encyclopedia of Cheerleading*, 13, 27.

73. Ibid., 215.

74. Hatton and Hatton, "The Sideline Show," 27.

2. Institutionalization and Commercialization

1. Sonja Steptoe, "The Pom-pom Chronicles," *Sports Illustrated* 75 (6 Jan. 1992), 40-41.

2. Westbrook Pegler in the *Chicago Tribune*, quoted in "Let Us Sigh for the Silenced Yell," *Literary Digest* 112 (2 Jan. 1932), 36.

3. "Cheer Leaders Will Receive Class Credit at Stanford," *New York Times*, 25 Jan. 1924, 13.

4. "The Broadening Curriculum," 16.

5. Turvold, *Art of Cheerleading*, 21.

6. Carl L. Amundson, "So You Want To Be a Cheerleader!" *School Activities* 22 (Nov. 1950), 88, 104.

7. M.L. Staples, "School Morale Through the Pep Assembly," *School Activities* 11 (Sept. 1939), 17.

8. F.B. Kutz, "Cheerleading Rules, Desirable Traits and Qualifications," *School Activities* 26 (May 1955), 310.

9. "Select Rally Squad on Sound Basis," *School Activities* 30 (Sept. 1958), 37.

10. Humphrey and Humphrey, *Cheerleading and Song Leading*, 11-12.

11. Neil, *Encyclopedia of Cheerleading*, 28.

12. Larry J. Weber and others, "Factors Related to Exclusion of Students from School Activities," ERIC, ED 204837 (1981), Abstract.

13. Neil, *Encyclopedia of Cheerleading*, 212.

14. Bob Livingston, "School Personnel Rehired," *Mt. Carmel (IL) Daily Republican Register*, 19 Mar. 1991, 1; Bob Livingston, "Cheerleader Selection Discussed," *Mt. Carmel (IL) Daily Republican Register*, 24 Apr. 1991, 1.

15. Sojka, "Evolution of the Student-Athlete," 59.

16. Pat Ryan, "Once It Was Only Sis-boom-bah! Collegiate Cheerleaders," *Sports Illustrated* 30 (6 Jan. 1969), 47.

17. Steve Cady, "Garden Echos With 18 Rah, Rah, Rahs for Tradition," *New York Times*, 18 Feb. 1972, 32.

18. "Cheerleader Dispute Is Settled; School Boycott in Illinois to End," *New York Times*, 20 Nov. 1967, 35.

19. Judy Klemesrud, "Still the Rah-Rah, But Some Aren't Cheering," *New York Times*, 11 Oct. 1971, 44.

20. "Owner of 3 Companies Is Leading in Cheers," *New York Times*, 28 Oct. 1972, 45.

21. Ibid.

22. Jeffrey Lee Brezner, "The Relationship of Administrative Practices and Procedures to the Integration of Desegregated Secondary Schools," ERIC, ED 124627 (1974), Abstract.

23. Thomas W. Collins, "Reconstructing a High School Society After Court-ordered Desegregation," ERIC, ED 151500 (1977), Abstract.

24. Jeannie Ralston, "Rah! Power," *Texas Monthly* 22 (Oct. 1994), 151.

25. "U. of Miss. Still Working to Drop Confederate Flag," *Chronicle of Higher Education*, 10 July 1991, A3.

26. "With Gusto: Cheerleaders from St. Joseph by the Sea High School Competing in the Fifth Annual Cheerleading Contest of the New York Catholic Youth Organizations," *New York Times*, 26 Feb. 1973, 35; "Program Scheduled for Cheerleaders," *New York Times*, 9 June 1974, NJ35.

27. Jonathan J. Brower, "Professionalization of Organized Youth Sport: Social Psychological Impacts and Outcomes," *American Academy of Political and Social Science. Annals* 445 (Sept. 1979), 40.

28. Sojka, "Evolution of the Student-Athlete," 61.

29. George Vecsey, "Young Footballers Getting Ready Too," *New York Times*, 21 Aug. 1973, 34; Bob Larkin, "21st YAFL Season About to Kick Off," *Albuquerque Journal*, 22 July 1987, C5; Richard Stevens, "Madhouse Football: Young America Football League Needs Bigger Place to Play," *Albuquerque Tribune*, 28 Oct. 1991, F6.

30. "Cheerleading Clinic," *Fayetteville (NC) Observer-Times*, 4 Aug. 1990, 18E; "Cheerleading for Teens," *Washington Post*, 2 Jan. 1992, Va.4;

"Cheerleading Club," *Fayetteville (NC) Observer-Times*, 4 Feb. 1989, 18E; Keith Baker, "Something Rotten About High School Sports (Cont'd.)," *Washington Post*, 18 July 1992, A19.

31. Loken, *Cheerleading*, 2nd ed., 76-78.

32. Charles E. Forsythe, *The Administration of High School Athletics* (New York: Prentice-Hall, 1948), 266.

33. Neil, *Encyclopedia of Cheerleading*, 111-14.

34. "Cobre's Cheerleaders Promoting Sportsmanship with a Video-tape," *Albuquerque Journal*, 5 Mar. 1989, E5.

35. Susie Gran, "Club, Private Company Offer APS Pay-for-Play After-school Programs," *Albuquerque Tribune*, 27 Apr. 1990, Al.

36. Peter Baker, "Fairfax Pares High School Athletics," *Washington Post*, 7 June 1991, B5.

37. Kate Nelson and Hank Stuever, "Tuition Hike Won't Alter UNM Bottom-of-Barrel Salary Stance," *Albuquerque Tribune*, 16 Apr. 1991, A5.

38. H. Appenzeller and C.T. Ross, "Minnesota—Cheerleader Awarded $200,200 for Injury Sustained in Accident," *Sports and the Courts* 6 (Fall 1985), 10-12.

39. Mike Kaemper, "Cheerleaders Won't Be Tested for Drugs," *New Mexico Daily Lobo*, 2 Feb. 1988, 1.

40. Turvold, *Art of Cheerleading*, 9.

41. John D. Flatt, "Cheerleaders Are the Glue Men; Magic Valley's Workshop," *Clearing House* 27 (Apr. 1953), 476.

42. Priscilla M. Bell, "But Can She Jump!" *School Activities* 40 (Jan. 1969), 8-9.

43. Neil, *Encyclopedia of Cheerleading*, 205.

44. S. Olcott, "Year-round Checklist for the Cheerleading Advisor; Part l," *Scholastic Coach* 47 (Jan. 1978), 104, 130–31; S. Olcott, "Year-round Checklist for the Cheerleading Advisor; Part 2," *Scholastic Coach* 47 (Feb. 1978), 91, 130–31; Chicago Board of Education, "Cheerleading: A Handbook for Teacher-Sponsors," ERIC, ED 243854 (1981).

45. Frank W. Mason, "Suggested Constitution for an Inter-scholastic Cheerleaders' Association," in *School Yells: Suggestions for Cheerleaders*, Lawrence M. Brings (Minneapolis: Northwestern Press, 1944), 43, 47.

46. Ibid., 47-48.

47. "State Cheerleading: Local Schools Earn Top Prizes," *Albuquerque Tribune*, 8 Apr. 1991, B3; "Cheer, Drill Teams Compete," *Albuquerque Journal*, 5 Apr. 1992, F6.

48. "Cheerleaders Honored," *Onawa (Iowa) Sentinel*, 31 May 1990, 7.

49. Jean K. Lundholm and John M. Littrell, "Desire for Thinness Among High-school Cheerleaders: Relationship to Disordered Eating and Weight Control Behaviors," *Adolescence* 21 (Fall 1986), 574.

50. Ibid., 576.

51. "The University of Connecticut Has Dropped Its Weight Limit for Female Cheerleaders," *Chronicle of Higher Education*, 4 Sept. 1991, A45.

52. John Spano, "School Gives Her Nothing to Cheer About," *Los Angeles Times*, 23 Oct. 1986, II 1, 5.

53. "Cheering Unlimited: In an Indiana School, Pom-pom Democracy," *People Weekly* 37 (10 Feb. 1992), 72.

54. Loken and Dypwick, *Cheerleading & Marching Bands*, xv.

55. Stella Spicer Gilb, *Cheerleading, Pep Clubs and Baton Twirling* (Lexington, KY: Hurst, 1955); *Cheerleading and Baton Twirling* (New York: Grosset & Dunlap, 1970); Humphrey and Humphrey, *Cheerleading and Song Leading*; L.R. Herkimer and Phyllis Hollander, eds., *The Complete Book of Cheerleading* (Garden City: Doubleday, 1975); Neil, *Encyclopedia of Cheerleading*; Barbara Egbert, *Cheerleading and Songleading* (New York: Sterling, 1980); Nancy L. Robison, *Cheerleading* (New York: Harvey House, 1980); Jim W. Hawkins, *Cheerleading Is For Me* (Minneapolis: Lerner, 1981); Randy Neil, *The Official Handbook of School Spirit* (New York: Simon and Schuster, 1981); Betty Lou Phillips, *Go! Fight! Win!: The National Cheerleaders Association Guide for Cheerleaders* (New York: Delacorte, 1981); Shan Finney, *Cheerleading and Baton Twirling* (New York: F. Watts, 1982); Rusty McKinley, *The Complete Partner Stunt Book* (Memphis: Regmar, 1982); Randy Neil, *The Official Pompon Girl's Handbook* (New York: St. Martin's/Marek, 1983); Barbara Egbert, *Action Cheerleading* (New York: Sterling, 1984); Elaine Hart and Judi Lamberth, *The Official Handbook for Cheerleader Sponsors* (Dubuque: Kendall/Hunt, 1985); Joseph M. Fodero and Ernest E. Furblur, *Creating Gymnastic Pyramids and Balances* (Champaign, IL: Human Kinetics, 1989).

56. Neil, *Encyclopedia of Cheerleading*, 13.

57. "Mr. Cheerleader," *American Magazine* 161 (Mar. 1956), 47.

58. "Key to Cheerleading: 'Big, Strong, Definite' Motions," *New York Times*, 21 Sept. 1967, 54.

59. Neil, *Encyclopedia of Cheerleading*, 241-42.

60. "Peptalk: Let's Hear It for Spirit!" *Teen* 28 (June 1984), 66.

61. *Fundamentals of Cheerleading* (Tulsa: Miracle Video, 1988); *Cheerleading and Dance* (Ann Arbor: Champions on Film); *Cheerleading by the Rules* (Kansas City: National Federation of State High School Associations, 1989); *Conditioning for Cheerleaders* (North Palm Beach, FL: Athletic Institute); *Cheerleading For the '90s* (Kansas City: National

Federation of State High School Associations, 1991); *Cheerleading Tryout Secrets* (Dallas: National Cheerleaders Association, 1987); *Dance/Drill Team Techniques* (Santa Monica: Ready Reference Press); *The Fundamentals of Cheerleading* (Shawnee Mission, KS: RMI Media Productions, 1981); *Universal Partner Stunts for Cheerleading* (Memphis: Universal Cheerleaders Association, 1984); *Universal Tumbling For Cheerleading* (Memphis: Universal Cheerleaders Association, 1984).

62. Gregory Curtis, "The Joy of Cheerleading," *Texas Monthly* 5 (Oct. 1977), 206.

63. Ibid., 207.

64. Cathy Marston, "Cheerleaders Display New Image, Organization," *Trinitonian*, Trinity University (San Antonio), 8 Sept. 1989, 3.

65. "Edgewood Holds Clinic for Cheerleaders," *Ohio Schools* 33 (May 1955), 20-21.

66. Pico Iyer, "In California: Catching the Spirit," *Time* 126 (12 Aug. 1985), 8.

67. "Owner of 3 Companies Is Leading in Cheers," 39.

68. Ibid.

69. Steptoe, "The Pom-pom Chronicles," 40.

70. Ibid., 43-44.

71. Ibid., 40, 43-44, 46.

72. Ibid., 40-41, 43.

73. Ibid., 46.

74. David Bourne, "Rah-Rah Becomes Booming Business," *Fayetteville (NC) Observer-Times*, 1 July 1990, 1H.

75. Alexander Douglas, "Sports Acrobatics and Cheerleaders," *International Gymnast* 24 (Mar. 1982), 42; advertisement for Gold Cup Gymnastic School cheerleading classes, *Albuquerque Journal*, 25 Aug. 1991, C8; advertisement for Omega Gymnastics cheerleading camp, *Fayetteville (NC) Observer-Times*, 28 July 1991, 5E.

76. "Fitness Center Helps Children Get in Shape," *Albuquerque Tribune*, 17 Dec. 1990, F3.

77. Cathy Smith, "The Cheer Career," *San Antonio (TX) Express-News Magazine*, 29 Sept. 1991, 17.

78. Janet Cawley, "Cheerleading Inspires Extreme Behavior in Texas," *Albuquerque Journal*, 30 Aug. 1991, B9.

79. "Cheerleader's Father Pleads Guilty to Writing Threats," *Washington Post*, 5 Nov. 1992, A7.

3. From Those Who Yell to Those Who Sell

1. Richard Whittingham, *The Washington Redskins: An Illustrated History* (New York: Simon and Schuster, 1990), 56.

2. "November Yells," 38.

3. James J. Haggerty, *"Hail to the Redskins": The Story of the Washington Redskins* (Washington, D.C.: Seven Seas, 1974), 44, 48, 56.

4. Alan Beall, *Braves on the Warpath: The Fifty Greatest Games in the History of the Washington Redskins* (Washington, D.C.: Kinloch, 1988), 7.

5. Gail Shister, "The Pro Football Cheerleaders: What They're Like, How Much They Make, How They Feel About All That Shake, Shake, Shake They Do," *Glamour* 79 (Feb. 1981), 166.

6. Interview with Stanley Hordes, former member of the Washington Redskins marching band, 27 Nov. 1992.

7. Whittingham, *The Washington Redskins*, 50; *The NFL's Official Encyclopedic History of Professional Football* (New York: Macmillan, 1977), 91.

8. John Hawkins, *Texas Cheerleaders: The Spirit of America* (New York: St. Martin's, 1991), 93-94.

9. Olivia Lane, ed., *The Official 1982 Dallas Cowboys Bluebook* (Dallas: Taylor, 1982), 115.

10. Bruce Newman, "Gimme an 'S', Gimme an 'E,' Gimme . . . : Cheerleaders for Pro Football Teams," *Sports Illustrated* 48 (22 May 1978), 18.

11. Edwin Shrake, "Trouping the Colors for Gussie Nell Davis; Kilgore Rangerettes, College Dance-drill Team," *Sports Illustrated* 41 (16 Dec. 1974), 48.

12. Ibid.; Hawkins, *Texas Cheerleaders*, 122.

13. Hawkins, *Texas Cheerleaders*, 121.

14. Stephanie Salter, "There's Gold in Them Nuggets; 49ers Promotional Singing and Dancing Group," *Sports Illustrated* 41 (23 Sept. 1974), 38.

15. Ibid.

16. Ibid., 38, 42.

17. Hawkins, *Texas Cheerleaders*, 94.

18. James Ward Lee, "Legends in Their Own Time: The Dallas Cowboy [sic] Cheerleaders," in *Legendary Ladies of Texas*, Francis Edward Abernethy, ed., *Publications of the Texas Folklore Society* 43 (1981), 197.

19. Hawkins, *Texas Cheerleaders*, 94.

20. Lane, *Official 1982 Dallas Cowboys Bluebook*, 115.

21. Hawkins, *Texas Cheerleaders*, 94.

22. *The Official 1981 Dallas Cowboys Bluebook* (Dallas: Taylor, 1981), 65.

23. Lane, *Official 1982 Dallas Cowboys Bluebook*, 114.

24. Ibid.

25. *Official 1981 Dallas Cowboys Bluebook*, 65.

26. Steve Cameron, "Romance Has Ended, Now It's Time to Kiss the Girls Goodbye," *Denver Post*, 5 Mar. 1980, 25.

27. Walter Leavy, "NFL Cheerleaders," *Ebony* 37 (Dec. 1981), 130.

28. Lee, "Legends in Their Own Time," 196.

29. Newman, "Gimme an 'S,'" 18.

30. Lee, "Legends in Their Own Time," 196; Leavy, "NFL Cheerleaders," 125.

31. "Razzle-dazzle; CBS Football Coverage," *Newsweek* 64 (28 Sept. 1964), 65.

32. Lissa Megan Morrow, "'38 . . . 24. . .36 . . . Hike!'" *Los Angeles* 25 (Nov. 1980), 130, 132.

33. Ibid., 132.

34. Newman, "Gimme an 'S,'" 18.

35. "Sex in the Locker Room, and on the Football Field, Fuels Old Controversy," *Jet* 55 (19 Oct. 1978), 46.

36. Newman, "Gimme an 'S,'" 19.

37. Dana Parsons, "Cheerleaders Lose Uniforms," *Denver Post*, 21 Nov. 1979, 2; Dana Parsons, "TD's Loss Becomes Playboy Readers' Gain," *Denver Post*, 25 Nov. 1979, 2.

38. "N.F.L: The Nubile Female League?" *Women's Sports* 1 (Feb. 1979), 12.

39. Jim Kirksey, "'Save the Pony Express' Campaign Begins," *Denver Post*, 4 Mar. 1980, 3.

40. Leavy, "NFL Cheerleaders," 125, 130.

41. Diane K. Shah, "Sis-Boom-Bah!" *Newsweek* 90 (7 Nov. 1977), 87.

42. Anne M. Peterson, "Emmy-winning, Double-platinum Paula Abdul Has an Itch to Act," *Albuquerque Tribune*, 27 Nov. 1989, B7.

43. *Morning Edition*, National Public Radio, 16 Nov. 1990.

44. Richard Rottkov, "The Great NASL Cheerleader Explosion: Boom or Bust?" *Soccer* 5 (Apr.-May 1979), 17; Richard Rottkov, "The Making of a Cosmos Girl," *Soccer* 5 (Apr.-May 1979), 20.

45. "Cheerleaders and Indoor Soccer," *Soccer News* 2 (Jan./Feb./ Mar. 1983), 8-9.

46. Judith Timson, "Bounce for Glory; Canadian Football League Cheerleaders," *Maclean's* 91 (21 Aug. 1978), 29-31.

47. Robert Wieder, "The First Hurrah; The Oakland Invaders Get a Cheerleading Squad—and How," *California Magazine* 8 (Apr. 1983), 68.

48. "Everett Leads Confident Rams into London," *Albuquerque Journal*, 4 Aug. 1987, C4.

49. Ibid.

50. Raymond Algar, "American Football," *Leisure Management* 8, no. 6 (1988), 58-59.

51. Mike Freeman, "WLAF May Not Be a Total Laugh," *Washington Post*, 27 Mar. 1991, Fl.

52. *Entertainment Tonight*, 4 May 1992.

53. *KGGM News*, Albuquerque, NM, 1 Feb. 1992.

54. Leavy, "NFL Cheerleaders," 128.

55. Janet Wiscombe, "Smiles Don't Express a Big Happy Family," *Denver Post*, 22 Nov. 1979, 56.

56. *Official 1981 Dallas Cowboys Bluebook*, 69-80.

57. Leavy, "NFL Cheerleaders," 126.

58. Judith Weinraub, "The Revolt of the Redskinettes," *Washington Post*, 20 Sept. 1992, F1; Joe Flower, "Survival of the Fittest," *Sport Magazine* 75 (Oct. l984), 94; Lana Henderson, "Cowboys Cheerleaders Building an Industry on the Dallas Woman," *Dallas Magazine* 57 (Sept. 1978), 20.

59. Leo Suarez, "A Conflict of Interest?" *Sporting News* 202 (3 Nov. 1986), 36.

60. *Official 1981 Dallas Cowboys Bluebook*, 68.

61. "Susie Walker Is First Cougar in the NFL," *(Kutztown, PA) Patriot*, 27 Dec. 1990, 1.

62. Peterson, "Emmy-winning, Double-platinum Paula Abdul," B7.

63. "Paula Abdul Tops MTV Awards as 'Straight Up' Wins 4 Times," *Fayetteville (NC) Observer*, 7 Sept. 1989.

64. "Susie Walker Is First Cougar," 1.

65. Suzette Scholz, *Deep in the Heart of Texas: Reflections of Former Dallas Cowboys Cheerleaders* (New York: St. Martin's, 1991), 21.

66. Shister, "The Pro Football Cheerleaders," 170.

67. Dana Parsons, "Ex-Pony Express Members Still Reliving Daze of Noise, Glamour," *Denver Post*, 2 Nov. 1980, 24.

68. Ibid.

69. Scholz, *Deep in the Heart of Texas*, 10.

70. Bruce Chadwick, "Big-time Cheerleaders," *Cosmopolitan* 193 (Oct. 1982), 122.

71. Tony Brenna and Angela Aiello, "Alan Thicke in Red-hot Secret Romance with a Cheerleader Half His Age," *National Enquirer*, 17 Mar. 1992, 24.

72. Scholz, *Deep in the Heart of Texas*, 64.

73. Shister, "The Pro Football Cheerleaders," 170.

74. Chadwick, "Big-time Cheerleaders," 122.

75. Scholz, *Deep in the Heart of Texas*, 72.

76. Chadwick, "Big-time Cheerleaders," 126.

77. John M. Crewdson, "Cheering for the Cowboys," *New York Times*, 19 Apr. 1978, C15.

78. "Some Names," *New Yorker* 59 (12 Dec. 1983), 47.

79. Lane, *Official 1982 Dallas Cowboys Bluebook*, 116.

80. Wieder, "The First Hurrah," 68.

81. Scholz, *Deep in the Heart of Texas*, 8.

82. Henderson, "Cowboys Cheerleaders Building an Industry," 19.

83. Ibid.; Rick Nathanson, "Ex-Eldorado Cheerleader Now Works for Pro Team," *Albuquerque Journal*, 23 Aug. 1988, B1.

84. Lane, *Official 1982 Dallas Cowboys Bluebook*, 117.

85. Hawkins, *Texas Cheerleaders*, 93.

86. Scholz, *Deep in the Heart of Texas*, 172.

87. Joan Zingelman, Letter to the Editor, *Denver Post*, 4 Mar. 1980, 15.

88. "Miami Dolphin Cheerleaders Model 'Love Me, Read to Me' T-Shirts," *American Libraries* 20 (Feb. 1989), 105.

89. Scholz, *Deep in the Heart of Texas*, 10, 97.

90. Flower, "Survival of the Fittest," 94.

91. Lee Ballard, "What a Job: Managing the Cowboys Cheerleaders," *Dallas Magazine* 16 (Jan. 1982), 58.

92. Hawkins, *Texas Cheerleaders*, 99.

93. Scholz, *Deep in the Heart of Texas*, 90.

94. M. Howard Gelfand, "Parkettes Today, But Lewdafisks Tomorrow?" *MPLS* (Minneapolis) 6 (Oct. 1978), 4.

95. Lane, *Official 1982 Dallas Cowboys Bluebook*, 120-28.

96. Steve Aschburner, "'Rollerdome' Is No Place for Football, Ditka Says," *Albuquerque Tribune*, 5 Dec. 1987, B4; Suzanne Malich, "Skate Firms Put Wheels on the Line," *Albuquerque Journal*, 9 Oct. 1988, D5.

97. Dana Parsons, "Petitions 'Won't Change' Pony Express Decision," *Denver Post*, 5 Mar. 1980, 20.

98. Ibid.

99. "N.F.L: The Nubile Female League?" 12.

100. Chadwick, "Big-time Cheerleaders," 127.

101. Ibid.

102. Scholz, *Deep in the Heart of Texas*, 238.

103. Chadwick, "Big-time Cheerleaders," 122.

104. Lane, *Official 1982 Dallas Cowboys Bluebook*, 114; Ballard, "What a Job," 59.

105. "Susie Walker Is First Cougar," 1.

106. Parsons, "Cheerleaders Lose Uniforms," 2.

107. Timson, "Bounce for Glory," 30.

108. Judith Weinraub, "Redskinettes See Red: Nepotism, Racism Alleged; Tryout to Be Boycotted," *Washington Post*, 22 Mar. 1990, C2; Weinraub, "The Revolt of the Redskinettes," F6.

109. Wiscombe, "Smiles Don't Express a Big Happy Family," 51.

110. Scholz, *Deep in the Heart of Texas*, 212.

111. Ibid., 190.

112. "Some Names," 47.

113. Shister, "The Pro Football Cheerleaders," 169.

114. Henderson, "Cowboys Cheerleaders Building an Industry," 20.

115. Scholz, *Deep in the Heart of Texas*, 157.

116. "Susie Walker Is First Couger," 7.

117. Henderson, "Cowboys Cheerleaders Building an Industry," 20.

118. "The NBA," *Albuquerque Tribune*, 28 Nov. 1991, C4.

119. Hawkins, *Texas Cheerleaders*, 97.

120. Scholz, *Deep in the Heart of Texas*, 225.

121. Ibid., 155, 159-60.

122. Shister, "The Pro Football Cheerleaders," 166; Weinraub, "The Revolt of the Redskinettes," F6.

123. Weinraub, "The Revolt of the Redskinettes," F6.

124. Scholz, *Deep in the Heart of Texas*, 140.

125. Weinraub, "The Revolt of the Redskinettes," F6.

126. Scholz, *Deep in the Heart of Texas*, 151.

127. Lane, *Official 1982 Dallas Cowboys Bluebook,* 117; Shister, "Pro Football Cheerleaders," 169.

128. Shister, "The Pro Football Cheerleaders," 169; Nathanson, "Ex-Eldorado Cheerleader," B7.

129. "3 Ex-Oiler Cheerleaders Sue the Team for $23.5 Million," *Jet* 69 (21 Oct. 1985), 47.

130. Shister, "The Pro Football Cheerleaders," 169.

131. Weinraub, "The Revolt of the Redskinettes," F6.

132. Hawkins, *Texas Cheerleaders*, 95.

133. Ibid.

134. Scholz, *Deep in the Heart of Texas*, 98-99.

135. Steve Daley, "Are the Redskinettes Prettier Than the Cowgirls? Are the Redskinettes Prettier Than the Redskins?" *Washingtonian* 13 (Sept. 1978), 138.

136. Shister, "The Pro Football Cheerleaders," 169.

137. Indianapolis Colts-Denver Broncos preseason game, televised 11 Aug. 1990.

138. *Official 1981 Dallas Cowboys Bluebook,* 67.

139. *KOAT News*, Albuquerque, NM, 28 Jan. 1993.

140. Weinraub, "The Revolt of the Redskinettes, F1.

141. Ibid., F6.

142. Scholz, *Deep in the Heart of Texas*, 142.

143. Molly Ivins, "As Thousands Cheer," *Progressive* 53 (Aug. 1989), 35.

144. "Cowboys Owner Loses to Cheerleaders," *Albuquerque Tribune*, 27 June 1989, B1.

145. Ivins, "As Thousands Cheer," 35.

146. Cameron, "Romance Has Ended," 25.

4. Content and Style

1. Gradler, *Psychology and Technique of Cheer-leading*, 12.

2. "Cheerleader News," *Onawa (IA) Sentinel*, 23 Aug. 1990, 2.

3. Loken and Dypwick, *Cheerleading & Marching Bands*, 46.

4. Smith, "The Cheer Career," 13.

5. Bob Anderson, ed., *Sportsource* (Mountain View, CA: World Publications, 1975), 117.

6. Turvold, *Art of Cheerleading*, 19.

7. Humphrey and Humphrey, *Cheerleading and Song Leading*, 44.

8. Loken and Dypwick, *Cheerleading & Marching Bands*, 54.

9. Gradler, *Psychology and Technique of Cheer-leading*, 47.

10. Loken and Dypwick, *Cheerleading & Marching Bands*, 36.

11. Gradler, *Psychology and Technique of Cheer-leading*, 9.

12. Loken and Dypwick, *Cheerleading & Marching Bands*, 52.

13. Humphrey and Humphrey, *Cheerleading and Song Leading*, 49-50.

14. Ibid., 72.

15. Gradler, *Psychology and Technique of Cheer-leading*, 67.

16. Loken, *Cheerleading*, 2nd ed., 14.

17. Gradler, *Psychology and Technique of Cheer-leading*, 25-26.

18. Ibid., 28, 30, 31.

19. Ibid., 33.

20. Loken, *Cheerleading*, 2nd ed., 3.

21. Humphrey and Humphrey, *Cheerleading and Song Leading*, 11.

22. Ibid., 16.

23. Loken and Dypwick, *Cheerleading & Marching Bands*, 9-10.

24. Turvold, *Art of Cheerleading*, 16.

25. Humphrey and Humphrey, *Cheerleading and Song Leading*, 113.

26. Neil, *Encyclopedia of Cheerleading*, 43.

27. Ibid., 61.

28. Ibid., 89.

29. Gradler, *Psychology and Technique of Cheer-leading*, 47.

30. Turvold, *Art of Cheerleading*, 60-61.

31. Loken and Dypwick, *Cheerleading & Marching Bands*, xii.

32. Neil, *Encyclopedia of Cheerleading*, 11.

33. Charles Kuralt, "Those Good Old Cheers Gone By," *Reader's Digest* 117 (Sept. 1980), 54-55.

34. Gradler, *Psychology and Technique of Cheer-leading*, 72.

35. Turvold, *Art of Cheerleading*, 71.

36. A variant of this cheer, ending "We're gonna be their boss one day," is reported in Jim Belshaw, "News—Good, Bad and Other," *Albuquerque Journal*, 4 Apr. 1993, C1.

37. Ryan, "Once It Was Only Sis-boom-bah!" 53-54.

38. Klemesrud, "Still the Rah-Rah," 44.

39. "Owner of 3 Companies Is Leading in Cheers," 45.

40. Ibid.; Klemesrud, "Still the Rah-Rah," 44.

41. Turvold, *Art of Cheerleading*, 33.

42. Gradler, *Psychology and Technique of Cheer-leading*, 49.

43. Ralph C. Shoenstein, "Fight, Fight, Fight in Moderation," *Saturday Evening Post* 248 (Oct. 1976), 62.

44. Photograph of Janesville (WI) High School cheerleaders in Gach, "The Case For and Against Girl Cheerleaders," 302.

45. Loken, *Cheerleading & Marching Bands*, 4.

46. Turvold, *Art of Cheerleading*, 35.

47. Loken, *Cheerleading*, 2nd ed., 16.

48. Kate Luger, personal communication, Apr. 1993.

49. Neil, *Encyclopedia of Cheerleading*, 12.

50. Gradler, *Psychology and Technique of Cheer-leading*, 49.

51. Brings, *School Yells*, 93, 111.

52. Neil, *Encyclopedia of Cheerleading*, 13.

53. Nathan Joseph and Nicholas Alex, "The Uniform: A Sociological Perspective," *American Journal of Sociology* 77 (Jan. 1972), 719.

54. Gradler, *Psychology and Technique of Cheer-leading*, 55.

55. Neil, *Encyclopedia of Cheerleading*, 13, 127.

56. Ibid., 127.

57. Ibid., 136.

58. Brings, *School Yells*, 144.

59. Loken, *Cheerleading & Marching Bands*, 36.

60. Ryan, "Once It Was Only Sis-boom-bah!" 49-50.

61. "Cheerleading: Memphis State Tigers Win 1984 NCA National Championships and $5,000," *International Gymnast* 26 (Mar. 1984), 62.

62. Smith, "The Cheer Career," 10.

63. "Cheerleading: Memphis State Tigers," 61.

64. Jerome Garcia, "The Spirit Team," *New Mexico Daily Lobo*, 29 Jan. 1990, 7.

65. Smith, "The Cheer Career," 13.

66. Televised performance of the Kilgore Rangerettes in Macy's Thanksgiving Day Parade, 26 Nov. 1992.

67. Raleigh D. Amyx, "National Gymnastics Catastrophic Injury Registry," *International Gymnast* 23, Technical Supplement 6 (May 1981), 44.

68. Ibid., 45.

69. Steptoe, "The Pom-pom Chronicles," 46.

70. Ricardo Gandara, "Cheerleaders Cheer for Less Dangerous Stunts," *Albuquerque Tribune*, 7 Jan. 1987, A1, A7.

71. Michael J. Garcia, "Pyramids to Fall," *New Mexico Daily Lobo*, 30 July 1987, 27.

72. Steptoe, "The Pom-pom Chronicles," 46.

73. Ibid.

74. C.E. Goodman, "Unusual Nerve Injuries in Recreational Activities," *American Journal of Sports Medicine* 11 (July/Aug. 1983), 224-27; R.W. Shields and I.B. Jacobs, "Median Palmer Digital Neuropathy in a Cheerleader," *Archives of Physical Medicine and Rehabilitation* 67 (Nov. 1986), 824-26; Jamshid Tehranzadeh, David A. Labosky and Orlando F. Gabriele, "Ganglion Cysts and Tear of Triangular Fibrocartilages of Both Wrists in a Cheerleader," *American Journal of Sports Medicine* 11 (Sept./Oct. 1983), 357-59.

75. Paul Eugene Bravender, "The Effect of Cheerleading on the Female Singing Voice" (Ph.D. diss., Michigan State University, 1977), Abstract.

76. Ibid., 15, 5, 39.

77. Monica Ann McHenry and Alan R. Reich, "Effective Airway Resistance and Vocal Sound Pressure Level in Cheerleaders with a History of Dysphonic Episodes," *Folia Phoniatrica* 37 (1985), 224.

78. Anderson, *Sportsource*, 117.

79. Alison Frankel, "Is Cheerleading Getting Too Dangerous?" *Seventeen* 46 (Sept. 1987), 56.

80. "Judson, Churchill Cheerleaders Capture Honors at National Competition," *San Antonio (TX) Express-News*, 30 Dec. 1992, 3B.

81. John K. Sampson, "Cheers for Best: Bernalillo Cheerleaders Have Eyes on Nationals," *Albuquerque Tribune*, 9 Feb. 1989, B4.

82. Anderson, *Sportsource*, 117.

83. "Cheerleading: Memphis State Tigers Win," 61.

84. Loken and Dypwick, *Cheerleading & Marching Bands*, xii.

85. Castro, *RPH-30: A Pom-pon Team*, 4.

86. Interview with Brian Hanson, Assistant Wrestling Coach, Adams City High School, Commerce City, CO, 20 July 1991.

87. Rachel Petty, Letter to the Editor, *Albuquerque Tribune*, 30 Apr. 1990, A6.

88. "Cheerleading: Memphis State Tigers Win," 63.

89. Frankel, "Is Cheerleading Getting Too Dangerous?" 56-57.

90. Steptoe, "The Pom-pom Chronicles," 40.

91. Frankel, "Is Cheerleading Getting Too Dangerous?" 60.

92. Gradler, *Psychology and Technique of Cheer-leading*, 6.

93. Klemesrud, "Still the Rah-Rah," 44.

94. David Driver, "Cheers: Washington-Lee Senior All-American Got an Early Start on the Sidelines," *Arlington (VA) Courier*, 14 Nov. 1990, 9.

95. Rodney Peele, "Wakefield Cheerleaders Top County," *(Arlington, VA) Sun Weekly*, 22 Nov. 1994, 5.

96. Tracey Secrest, "Competing Cheerleaders?" *York (PA) Sunday News*, 2 Dec. 1990, A6.

97. Ibid.

98. William A. Reid, Letter to Sports Editor, *Albuquerque Tribune*, 2 June 1989, C10.

99. Gary Moss, "Fort Bragg Schools Plan Sports Teams," *Fayetteville (NC) Observer*, 29 Aug. 1989.

100. Janice Kaplan, "Jeers for Cheerleaders," *Seventeen* 36 (Oct. 1977), 42.

101. Stephen Buckley, "Panel Urges Making Cheerleading a Sport," *Washington Post*, 15 Dec. 1992, A8.

102. Bernice R. Sandler, *The Restoration of Title IX: Implications for Higher Education* (Washington, D.C.: Project on the Status and Education of Women, Association of American Colleges, 1989), 5.

103. "The New Faces of School Spirit," *UCLA Magazine* 2 (Summer 1990), 71.

5. On the Sidelines and in the Headlines

1. Kathleen Cushman, "Three Cheers For My Daughter," *New York Times Magazine*, 23 Oct. 1988, 28.

2. Quoted in Ivins, "As Thousands Cheer," 35.

3. Anna Quindlen, "Little League's Lot Better Now When Pitcher's a Girl," *Albuquerque Tribune*, 28 June 1988, D2.

4. Donnie Radcliffe, "Festivities Fit For a Queen: Pomp & Circumstance Aplenty for Elizabeth II's Visit," *Washington Post*, 13 May 1991, B8.

5. Erma Bombeck, "Do Babies Live Up to Names? Best Ask Vanna, Fawn or Ron," *Albuquerque Tribune*, 13 July 1987, B3.

6. Review of *Cheerleaders Can't Afford To Be Nice* in Linda Barrett Osborne, "Novel Reading," *Washington Post Book World*, 6 Jan. 1991, 8.

7. "Teen Births Stir Debate on Policies: Youths Account For 25% of All U.S. Abortions," *Albuquerque Journal*, 8 Nov. 1987, B1.

8. "Pregnant Cheerleaders Raise Fuss," *San Antonio (TX) Express-News*, 10 Oct. 1993, 1D.

9. Ed Schafer, "Former Poet Laureate Dies of Cancer at 71," *Albuquerque Journal*, 7 July 1991, E16.

10. Neil, *Encyclopedia of Cheerleading*, 26.

11. Gradler, *Psychology and Technique of Cheer-leading*, 24.

12. Sarah Booth Conroy, "The GOP's School for Spouses: Melinda Farris, Helping the Helpmates," *Washington Post*, 12 Aug. 1988, B1.

13. Mike Keefe, editorial cartoon, *Fayetteville (NC) Observer*, 6 Aug. 1990, 14A.

14. Marilyn Gardner, "Ms. Magazine at 15: Issues Change, Not Theme," *Albuquerque Journal*, 27 July 1987, B3.

15. Henry Payne, editorial cartoon, *Albuquerque Tribune*, 27 Oct. 1987, A6.

16. Gary Alan Fine with Bruce Noel Johnson, "The Promiscuous Cheerleader: An Adolescent Male Belief Legend," in *Manufacturing Tales: Sex and Money in Contemporary Legends*, Gary Alan Fine (Knoxville: University of Tennessee Press, 1992), 65.

17. Tom Batiuk, "Funky Winkerbean," comic strip, *Albuquerque Journal*, 16 Dec. 1990, unpaged.

18. Lynn Minton, "Fresh Voices," *Parade Magazine*, 4 Oct. 1992, 26.

19. Greg Evans, "Luann," comic strip, *Albuquerque Journal*, 16 Sept. 1987, D12.

20. Lewis Grizzard, "Are You a Bimbo? Does Your Name End in 'i'?" *Albuquerque Tribune*, 13 Oct. 1987, C2.

21. Nicole Hollander, "Sylvia," comic strip, *(Arlington, VA) Journal*, 24 June 1992, D3.

22. Berke Breathed, "Bloom County," comic strip, *New Mexico Daily Lobo*, 15 Sept. 1987, 4.

23. Fine and Johnson, "The Promiscuous Cheerleader," 60.

24. Ibid., 63-64.

25. William H. Swatos, Jr., "On Being Virgin: Theories and Data," *International Journal of Women's Studies* 4 (Nov.-Dec. 1981), 517-26.

26. Tom Batiuk, "Funky Winkerbean," comic strip, *Albuquerque Journal*, 23 Oct. 1987, E8.

27. John Louthan, "Briefcase," cartoon, *Albuquerque Tribune*, 21 Mar. 1988, C4.

28. Hal Hinson, "New on Video," *Washington Post*, 24 Dec. 1992, C7.

29. Hank Burchard, "Corcoran Duo's Feminist Charge," *Washington Post Weekend*, 3 Jan. 1992, 41.

30. Charles I. Glicksberg, "Extracurricular Activities and School Morale," *American School Board Journal* 110 (May 1945), 36.

31. Richard Wolkomir, "American Sign Language: 'It's Not Mouth Stuff—It's Brain Stuff,'" *Smithsonian* 23 (July 1992), 34; Greg Lopez, "You Don't Have to Hear to Cheer," *(Denver) Rocky Mountain News*, 31 Jan. 1993, 10-12.

32. Jerry Kirshenbaum, "They Thought They Could . . . and They Did!" *Sports Illustrated* 60 (19 Mar. 1984), 18.

33. James Yodice, "Exodus From Mountainair Changed Football Forever," *Albuquerque Journal*, 16 Oct. 1988, E1.

34. Children's Defense Fund, Publications catalog, (Washington, D.C.: CDF, Winter 1988/1989), unpaged.

35. Carol Morse, *Three Cheers for Polly* (Garden City: Doubleday, 1967); Frank Bonham, *Gimme an H, Gimme an E, Gimme an L, Gimme a P* (New York: Scribner, 1980); Norma Klein, *The Cheerleader* (New York: Knopf, 1985); Jennifer Sarasin, *Cheating* (New York: Scholastic, 1985); Ellen Leroe, *Have a Heart, Cupid Delaney!* (New York: Lodestar Books, 1986).

36. Susan Dodge, "Harvard Students with an Intellectual Bent Create a 'Support Group for Nerds,'" *Chronicle of Higher Education*, 9 May 1990, A1, A36.

37. Rita Kempley, "Land of Dashed Dreams," *Washington Post*, 6 Feb. 1988, G5.

38. Target advertising insert, *Albuquerque Journal*, 23 May 1993, 21; Toys "R" Us advertising insert, *Albuquerque Journal*, 23 Oct. 1989, 8R.

39. Wal-Mart advertising insert, *Albuquerque Journal*, 2 Aug. 1992, 23.

40. Miles Kimball catalog (Oskosh, WI: Miles Kimball Co., Fall, 1991), 87.

41. "Let's Hear It for Pep Squad Beauty," *Teen* 27 (Sept. 1983), 95.

42. Ron Lynch, "That's the Spirit!" *Seventeen* 44 (Aug. 1985), 352-57.

43. Lillian Vernon catalog (Virginia Beach, VA: Lillian Vernon, 1992), S4.

44. Television advertisement for Krystal's NFL Shop, Albuquerque, NM, c. 1990; The Official Big Red Gift Center catalog (Bloomington, IN: Indiana University, n.d.).

45. Dick Foster, "Disguised Cheerleader on Probation," *Albuquerque Tribune*, 5 Feb. 1991, D7; "The She on Prep Cheerleading Squad Was a 26-year-old He," *Albuquerque Tribune*, 20 Sept. 1990, A4.

46. "Mom Pleads Innocent in Hitman Case," *Albuquerque Journal* 1 Mar. 1991, A2; "'Stage-Mom' Gets 15 Years for Death Plot," *Albuquerque Tribune*, 5 Sept. 1991, C3; "Cheerleader Mom Critical of First Television Portrayal," *San Antonio (TX) Express-News*, 10 Nov. 1992, 15D; "Texas 'Cheerleader Mom' To Get New Murder-for-hire Trial," *Albuquerque Tribune*, 14 Oct. 1994, A4.

47. "Willing to Kill," *Washington Post*, 7 Nov. 1992, G5.

48. Robert Troidl and Sarah Peterson, "Mesa Public Schools: As Seen Through the Eyes of 1982–83 Seniors," ERIC, ED 249236 (1983), Abstract.

49. Ryan, "Once It Was Only Sis-boom-bah!" 50-51.

50. Mary-Ellen Banashek, "Memoirs of an Ex-cheerleader," *Mademoiselle* 82 (June 1976), 18.

51. Annette Carlson, personal communication, 1990.

52. Arlene Adcock, personal communication, 1990.

53. Huldah McQuillen, personal communication, 1990.

54. Nancy Fearheiley, personal communication, 1991.

55. Michael Ryan, "Here, Everybody Gets to Play," *Parade Magazine,* 15 Mar. 1992, 10.

56. Carlos Salazar, "Ex-cheerleader, Teacher 'Grego' Pino Dies at 58," *Albuquerque Tribune,* 13 July 1989, D2; "Paulette Marie Howell," obituary, *Washington Post,* 28 Dec. 1990, F4; "Judi Hamrick To Be Bride of Gregg Underwood," *Washington Post,* 18 Oct. 1989, B7.

57. Nancy Collins, "Girls of Autumn; for Ex-cheerleaders, the Pom-poms Sag, But Life Goes On," 221-22, 224-25.

58. Patrick Duffy, appearance on the *Tonight Show,* 22 July 1987.

59. Dominick Dunne, "The Light of Hussein," *Vanity Fair* 54 (Jan. 1991), 62; *Entertainment Tonight,* television program, 30 Aug. 1991; "15 Celebrities Who Were Cheerleaders," *Parade Magazine,* 29 Aug. 1993, 16; "Focus on Cheerleading," *Seventeen* 42 (Sept. 1983), 95; "The 'In' Crowd," *Self* Vol. 15 (Oct. 1993), 48; Ralph Keyes, "Rah! Rah! What? They Didn't Make Cheerleader," *Cosmopolitan* 196 (Mar. 1984), 170; Jim Leggett, "The Girl-Next-Door You Love to Have for Breakfast," *Star,* 28 May 1991, 16; "No Kidding? Facts About Some Famous Folks," *Albuquerque Tribune,* 5 Aug. 1991, A2; Sue Anne Pressley, "Texas Steel, Senate-Ready," *Washington Post,* 14 June 1993, Dl; David Wallechinsky and Amy Wallace, *The People's Almanac Presents the Book of Lists: The '90s Edition* (Boston: Little, Brown, 1993), 421-22; Gary Wills, *Reagan's America: Innocents at Home* (Garden City: Doubleday, 1987), 55.

60. Keyes, "Rah! Rah! What? They Didn't Make Cheerleader," 168.

61. Tom Seligson, "The Truth About Jane Pauley," *Parade Magazine,* 20 Sept. 1987, 5.

62. Kim Cunningham, "Chatter," *People Weekly* 39 (19 Apr. 1993), 114.

63. Barbara Roessner, "Are Cheerleaders on the Way Out?" Reprinted from the *Hartford Courant* in *The World,* 1 Oct. 1989, 3.

64. Ibid.

65. Georgia Dullea, "There's Always Something to Cheer About at Cheerleader Camp," *New York Times,* 2 Sept. 1975, 26.

66. Bunny Hoest and John Reiner, "Laugh Parade," cartoon, *Parade Magazine,* 21 June 1992, 12.

67. Lynn Johnston, "For Better or For Worse," comic strip, *Albuquerque Tribune*, 30 Jan. 1990, D6.

68. Terry Frei, "Demon Girls Cheer, Eye Championship," *Denver Post*, 10 Mar. 1978, 24.

69. Greg Webb, "Cheerleaders—Spirit Leaders and Then Some!" *Interscholastic Athletic Administration* 11 (Fall 1984), 19.

6. Thinking About Cheerleading

1. George Kurman, "What Does Girls' Cheerleading Communicate?" *Journal of Popular Culture* 20 (Fall 1986), 63.

2. Jay J. Coakley, *Sport in Society: Issues and Controversies,* 4th ed. (St. Louis: Times Mirror/Mosby, 1990), 218.

3. Laurel R. Davis, "Male Cheerleaders and the Naturalization of Gender" in *Sport, Men, and the Gender Order: Critical Feminist Perspectives,* Michael A. Messner and Donald F. Sabo, eds. (Champaign, IL: Human Kinetics, 1990), 160. .

Bibliography

Books

Anderson, Bob, ed. *Sportsource*. Mountain View, CA: World Publications, 1975.

Beall, Alan. *Braves on the Warpath: The Fifty Greatest Games in the History of the Washington Redskins*. Washington, D.C.: Kinloch, 1988.

Bonham, Frank. *Gimme an H, Gimme an E, Gimme an L, Gimme a P*. New York: Scribner, 1980.

Bravender, Paul Eugene. "The Effect of Cheerleading on the Female Singing Voice." Ph.D. dissertation, Michigan State University, 1977.

Brings, Lawrence M. *School Yells: Suggestions for Cheerleaders*. Minneapolis: Northwestern Press, 1944.

Castro, Orlino. *RPH-30: A Pom-pon Team*. Hawaiian Gardens, CA: J. Witherspoon Publications, 1975.

Cheerleading and Baton Twirling. New York: Grosset & Dunlap, 1970.

Coakley, Jay J. *Sport in Society: Issues and Controversies*, 4th ed. St. Louis: Times Mirror/Mosby, 1990.

Davis, Laurel R. "Male Cheerleaders and the Naturalization of Gender." In *Sport, Men, and the Gender Order: Critical Feminist Perspectives*, edited by Michael A. Messner and Donald F. Sabo, 153-61. Champaign, IL: Human Kinetics, 1990.

D'Emilio, John, and Estelle B. Freedman. *Intimate Matters: A History of Sexuality in America*. New York: Harper & Row, 1988.

Egbert, Barbara. *Action Cheerleading*. New York: Sterling, 1984.

——. *Cheerleading and Songleading*. New York: Sterling, 1980.

Fass, Paula S. *The Damned and the Beautiful: American Youth in the 1920's*. Oxford: Oxford University Press, 1979.

Fine, Gary Alan, with Bruce Noel Johnson. "The Promiscuous Cheerleader: An Adolescent Male Belief Legend." In *Manufacturing Tales: Sex and Money in Contemporary Legends*, 59-68. Knoxville: University of Tennessee Press, 1992.

Finney, Shan. *Cheerleading and Baton Twirling*. New York: F. Watts, 1982.

Fodero, Joseph M., and Ernest E. Furblur. *Creating Gymnastic Pyramids and Balances*. Champaign, IL: Human Kinetics, 1989.

Forsythe, Charles E. *The Administration of High School Athletics*. New York: Prentice-Hall, 1948.

147

Gilb, Stella Spicer. *Cheerleading, Pep Clubs and Baton Twirling*. Lexington, KY: Hurst Printing, 1955.

Gradler, Frank A. *Psychology and Technique of Cheer-leading: A Handbook for Cheer-leaders*. Menomonie, WI: Menomonie Athletic Book Supply, 1927.

Haggerty, James J. *"Hail to the Redskins": The Story of the Washington Redskins*. Washington, D.C.: Seven Seas, 1974.

Hart, Elaine, and Judi Lamberth. *The Official Handbook for Cheerleader Sponsors*. Dubuque, IA: Kendall/Hunt, 1985.

Hawkins, Jim W. *Cheerleading Is For Me*. Minneapolis: Lerner Publications, 1981.

Hawkins, John. *Texas Cheerleaders: The Spirit of America*. New York: St. Martin's Press, 1991.

Herkimer, L.R., and Phyllis Hollander, eds. *The Complete Book of Cheerleading*. Garden City: Doubleday, 1975.

Hoffman, Frank W., and William G. Bailey. *Sports & Recreation Fads*. New York: Haworth Press, 1991.

Horowitz, Helen Lefkowitz. *Campus Life: Undergraduate Cultures from the End of the Eighteenth Century to the Present*. New York: Alfred A. Knopf, 1987.

Humphrey, Marylou, and Ron Humphrey. *Cheerleading and Song Leading*. Rutland, VT: Charles E. Tuttle, 1970.

Kane, Joseph Nathan. *Facts About the Presidents*, 5th ed. New York: H.W. Wilson, 1989.

Klein, Norma. *The Cheerleader*. New York: Knopf, 1985.

Lane, Olivia, ed. *The Official 1982 Dallas Cowboys Bluebook*. Dallas: Taylor, 1982.

Leroe, Ellen. *Have a Heart, Cupid Delaney!* New York: Lodestar Books, 1986.

Loken, Newt, and Otis Dypwick. *Cheerleading & Marching Bands*. New York: Ronald Press, 1945.

Loken, Newt. *Cheerleading*, 2nd ed. Malabar, FL: Krieger, 1983. Reprint of 1961 ed.

Mason, Frank W. "Suggested Constitution For an Interscholastic Cheerleaders' Association." In *School Yells: Suggestions for Cheerleaders*, Lawrence M. Brings, 43-48. Minneapolis: Northwestern Press, 1944.

McKinley, Rusty. *The Complete Partner Stunt Book*. Memphis, TN: Regmar, 1982.

Morrison, Gertrude W. *The Girls of Central High at Basketball, or, The Great Gymnasium Mystery*. Akron, OH: Saalfield Publishing, 1914.

Morse, Carol. *Three Cheers for Polly*. Garden City: Doubleday, 1967.

Neil, Randy. *The Encyclopedia of Cheerleading*, 3rd ed. Shawnee Mission, KS: International Cheerleading Foundation, 1975.

——. *The Official Handbook of School Spirit*. New York: Simon and Schuster, 1981.

——. *The Official Pompon Girl's Handbook*. New York: St. Martin's/Marek, 1983.

The NFL's Official Encyclopedic History of Professional Football. New York: Macmillan, 1977.

The Official 1981 Dallas Cowboys Bluebook. Dallas: Taylor, 1981.

Palmatier, Robert A., and Harold L. Ray. *Sports Talk: A Dictionary of Sports Metaphors*. New York: Greenwood Press, 1989.

Phillips, Betty Lou. *Go! Fight! Win!: The National Cheerleaders Association Guide For Cheerleaders*. New York: Delacorte Press, 1981.

Rader, Benjamin G. *American Sports: From the Age of Folk Games to the Age of Spectators*. Englewood Cliffs: Prentice-Hall, 1983.

Robison, Nancy L. *Cheerleading*. New York: Harvey House, 1980.

Saiter, Susan. *Cheerleaders Can't Afford To Be Nice: A Novel*. New York: Donald I. Fine, 1990.

Sandler, Bernice R. *The Restoration of Title IX: Implications for Higher Education*. Washington, D.C.: Project on the Status and Education of Women, Association of American Colleges, 1989.

Sarasin, Jennifer. *Cheating*. New York: Scholastic, 1985.

Scholz, Suzette. *Deep In the Heart of Texas: Reflections of Former Dallas Cowboys Cheerleaders*. New York: St. Martin's Press, 1991.

Singer, Janet. *Cheer Leader*. Chicago: Goldsmith, 1934.

Solomon, Barbara M. *In the Company of Educated Women: A History of Women and Higher Education in America*. New Haven: Yale University Press, 1985.

Turvold, Bruce A. *The Art of Cheerleading*. Minneapolis: Northwestern Press, 1948.

Villarreal, Cindy. *The Cheerleader's Guide to Life*. New York: HarperPerennial, 1994.

Wallechinsky, David, and Amy Wallace. *The People's Almanac Presents the Book of Lists: The '90s Edition*. Boston: Little, Brown, 1993.

Whittingham, Richard. *The Washington Redskins: An Illustrated History*. New York: Simon and Schuster, 1990.

Wills, Garry. *Reagan's America: Innocents at Home*. Garden City: Doubleday, 1987.

York, George M., and Harry Hammer Clark. *Just Yells: A Guide for Cheer Leaders*. Syracuse, NY: Willis N. Bugbee Co., 1927.

Articles and Other Sources

Algar, Raymond. "American Football." *Leisure Management* (Herts, England) 8 (1988): 58-59.

"All-America." *Time* 34 (11 Dec. 1939): 42.

American Graffiti, 35 mm, 110 min., Universal-Lucasfilm Ltd.-Coppola Production, 1973.

Amundson, Carl L. "So You Want To Be a Cheerleader!" *School Activities* 22 (Nov. 1950): 88.

Amyx, Raleigh D. "National Gymnastics Catastrophic Injury Registry." *International Gymnast* 23, Technical Supplement 6 (May 1981): TS 44-47.

Andrus, Ethel Percy. "School Spirit." *National Education Association. Proceedings and Addresses* (1917): 528-30.

Appenzeller, H., and C.T. Ross. "Minnesota—Cheerleader Awarded $200,200 for Injury Sustained in Accident." *Sports and the Courts* 6 (Fall 1985): 10-12.

Aschburner, Steve. "'Rollerdome' Is No Place for Football, Ditka Says." *Albuquerque Tribune,* 5 Dec. 1987: B4.

Baker, Keith. "Something Rotten About High School Sports (Cont.)." *Washington Post,* 18 July 1992: A19.

Baker, Peter, "Fairfax Pares High School Athletics." *Washington Post,* 7 June 1991: B5.

Ballard, Lee. "What a Job: Managing the Cowboys Cheerleaders." *Dallas Magazine* 16 (Jan. 1982): 58.

Banashek, Mary-Ellen. "Memoirs of an Ex-cheerleader." *Mademoiselle* 82 (June 1976): 18.

Batiuk, Tom. "Funky Winkerbean," comic strip. *Albuquerque Journal,* 23 Oct. 1997: E8.

——. "Funky Winkerbean," comic strip. *Albuquerque Journal,* 16 Dec. 1990: unpaged.

Bell, Priscilla M. "But Can She Jump!" *School Activities* 40 (Jan. 1969): 8-9.

Belshaw, Jim. "News—Good, Bad and Other." *Albuquerque Journal,* 4 Apr. 1993: C1.

Bombeck, Erma. "Do Babies Live Up to Names? Best Ask Vanna, Fawn or Ron." *Albuquerque Tribune,* 13 July 1987: B3.

Bourne, David. "Rah-Rah Becomes Booming Business." *Fayetteville (NC) Observer-Times,* 1 July 1990: 1H.

Breathed, Berke. "Bloom County," comic strip. *New Mexico Daily Lobo,* 15 Sept. 1987: 4.

Brenna, Tony, and Angela Aiello. "Alan Thicke in Red-hot Secret Romance with a Cheerleader Half His Age." *National Enquirer,* 17 Mar. 1992: 24.

Brezner, Jeffrey Lee. "The Relationship of Administrative Practices and Procedures to the Integration of Desegregated Secondary Schools." ERIC, ED 124627 (1974), Abstract.

"The Broadening Curriculum." *New York Times*, 25 Jan. 1924: 16.

Brower, Jonathan J. "Professionalization of Organized Youth Sport: Social Psychological Impacts and Outcomes." *American Academy of Political and Social Science. Annals* 445 (Sept. 1979): 39-46.

Buckley, Stephen. "Panel Urges Making Cheerleading a Sport." *Washington Post*, 15 Dec. 1992: A8.

Buffy, the Vampire Slayer, 35 mm, 85 mins., 20th Century Fox, 1992.

Burchard, Hank. "Corcoran Duo's Feminist Charge." *Washington Post Weekend*, 3 Jan. 1992: 41.

Cady, Steve. "Garden Echos With 18 Rah, Rah, Rahs for Tradition." *New York Times*, 18 Feb. 1972: 32.

Cameron, Steve. "Romance Has Ended, Now It's Time to Kiss the Girls Goodbye." *Denver Post*, 5 Mar. 1980: 25.

Cawley, Janet. "Cheerleading Inspires Extreme Behavior in Texas." *Albuquerque Journal*, 30 Aug. 1991: B9.

Chadwick, Bruce. "Big-time Cheerleaders." *Cosmopolitan* 193 (Oct. 1982): 122.

"Cheer, Drill Teams Compete." *Albuquerque Journal*, 5 Apr. 1992: F6.

"Cheer Leaders Will Receive Class Credit at Stanford." *New York Times*, 25 Jan. 1924: 13.

"Cheering Unlimited: In an Indiana School, Pom-pom Democracy." *People Weekly* 37 (10 Feb. 1992): 72.

"Cheerleader Dispute Is Settled; School Boycott in Illinois to End. *New York Times*, 20 Nov. 1967: 35.

"Cheerleader Mom Critical of First Television Portrayal." *San Antonio (TX) Express-News*, 10 Nov. 1992: 15D.

"Cheerleader News." *Onawa (IA) Sentinel*, 23 Aug. 1990: 2.

The Cheerleaders, 35 mm, The Cheerleaders Co., 1972.

"Cheerleaders & Indoor Soccer: Soccer American Style." *Soccer News (Canada)* 2 (Jan./Feb./Mar. 1983): 8-9.

"Cheerleader's Father Pleads Guilty to Writing Threats." *Washington Post*, 5 Nov. 1992: A7.

"Cheerleaders Honored." *Onawa (IA) Sentinel*, 31 May 1990: 7.

Cheerleaders Wild Weekend, 35 mm, Dimension Pictures, 1985.

Cheerleading and Dance, video. Ann Arbor: Champions on Film, n.d.

Cheerleading by the Rules, video. Kansas City, MO: National Federation of State High School Associations, 1989.

"Cheerleading Clinic." *Fayetteville (NC) Observer-Times*, 4 Aug. 1990: 18E.

"Cheerleading Club." *Fayetteville (NC) Observer-Times*, 4 Feb. 1989: 18E.

"Cheerleading for Teens." *Washington Post,* 2 Jan. 1992: Va.4.

Cheerleading for the '90s, video. Kansas City, MO: National Federation of State High School Associations, 1991.

"Cheerleading: Memphis State Tigers Win 1984 NCA National Championships and $5,000." *International Gymnast* 26 (Mar. 1984): 61-65.

Cheerleading Tryout Secrets, video. Dallas: National Cheerleaders Association, 1987.

Chicago Board of Education. "Cheerleading: A Handbook for Teacher-Sponsors." ERIC, ED 243854 (1981), Abstract.

Children's Defense Fund. Publications catalog. Washington, D.C.: CDF, Winter 1988/1989.

"Cobre's Cheerleaders Promoting Sportsmanship with a Videotape." *Albuquerque Journal,* 5 Mar. 1989: E5.

Collins, Nancy. "Girls of Autumn: For Ex-cheerleaders, the Pom-poms Sag But Life Goes On." *Esquire* 82 (Oct. 1974): 221-25.

Collins, Thomas W. "Reconstructing a High School Society After Court-ordered Desegregation." ERIC, ED 151500 (1977), Abstract.

Conditioning for Cheerleaders, video. North Palm Beach, FL: Athletic Institute, n.d.

Conroy, Sarah Booth. "The GOP's School for Spouses: Melinda Farris, Helping the Helpmates." *Washington Post,* 12 Aug. 1988: B1, B8.

Coughlin, Ellen K. "Scholars in the Humanities Are Disheartened by the Course of Debate Over Their Disciplines." *Chronicle of Higher Education,* 13 Sept. 1989: A2, A14.

"Cowboys Owner Loses to Cheerleaders." *Albuquerque Tribune,* 27 June 1989: B1.

Cowley, W.H. "Explaining the Rah Rah Boy." *New Republic* 46 (14 Apr. 1926): 242-45.

Crewdson, John M. "Cheering for the Cowboys." *New York Times,* 19 Apr. 1978: C1, C15.

Cunningham, Kim. "Chatter." *People Weekly* 39 (19 Apr. 1993): 114.

Curtis, Gregory. "The Joy of Cheerleading." *Texas Monthly* 5 (Oct. 1977): 108.

Cushman, Kathleen. "Three Cheers For My Daughter." *New York Times Magazine,* 23 Oct. 1988: 26-28.

Daley, Steve. "Are the Redskinettes Prettier Than the Cowgirls? Are the Redskinettes Prettier Than the Redskins?" *Washingtonian* 13 (Sept. 1978): 138.

Dance/Drill Team Techniques, video. Santa Monica, CA: Ready Reference Press, n.d.

Dodge, Susan. "Harvard Students with an Intellectual Bent Create a 'Support Group for Nerds.'" *Chronicle of Higher Education,* 9 May 1990: A1, A36.

Douglas, Alexander. "Sports Acrobatics and Cheerleaders." *International Gymnast* 24 (Mar. 1982): 42-43.

Driver, David. "Cheers: Washington-Lee Senior All-American Got an Early Start on the Sidelines." *Arlington (VA) Courier,* 14 Nov. 1990: 9.

Dullea, Georgia. "There's Always Something to Cheer About at Cheerleader Camp." *New York Times,* 2 Sept. 1975: 26.

Dunne, Dominick. "The Light of Hussein." *Vanity Fair* 54 (Jan. 1991): 58-65, 112-14.

"Edgewood Holds Clinic for Cheerleaders." *Ohio Schools* 33 (May 1955): 20-21.

Evans, Greg. "Luann," comic strip. *Albuquerque Journal,* 16 Sept. 1987: D12.

"Everett Leads Confident Rams into London." *Albuquerque Journal,* 4 Aug. 1987: C4.

"15 Celebrities Who Were Cheerleaders." *Parade Magazine,* 29 Aug. 1993: 16.

"Fitness Center Helps Children Get in Shape." *Albuquerque Tribune,* 17 Dec. 1990: F3.

Flatt, John D. "Cheerleaders Are the Glue Men: Magic Valley's Workshop." *Clearing House* 27 (Apr. 1953): 475-77.

Flower, Joe. "Survival of the Fittest." *Sport Magazine* 75 (Oct. 1984): 94.

"Focus on Cheerleading." *Seventeen* 42 (Sept. 1983): 94-95.

Fonssagrives, Mia. "Speaking of Pictures." *Life* 37 (25 Oct. 1954): 10-11.

Foster, Dick. "Disguised Cheerleader on Probation." *Albuquerque Tribune,* 5 Feb. 1991: D7.

Foster, William T. "Athletics by Proxy." *School and Society* 1 (22 May 1915): 733-38.

Frankel, Alison. "Is Cheerleading Getting Too Dangerous?" *Seventeen* 46 (Sept. 1987): 56.

Freeman, Mike. "WLAF May Not Be a Total Laugh." *Washington Post,* 27 Mar. 1991: F1.

Frei, Terry. "Demon Girls Cheer, Eye Championship." *Denver Post,* 10 Mar. 1978: 24.

The Fundamentals of Cheerleading, video. Shawnee Mission, KS: RMI Media Productions, 1981.

Fundamentals of Cheerleading, video. Tulsa: Miracle Video, 1988.

Gach, John J. "The Case For and Against Girl Cheerleaders." *School Activities* 9 (Mar. 1938): 301-02.

Gandara, Ricardo. "Cheerleaders Cheer For Less Dangerous Stunts." *Albuquerque Tribune,* 7 Jan. 1987: A7.

Garcia, Jerome. "The Spirit Team." *New Mexico Daily Lobo,* 29 Jan. 1990: 7.

Garcia, Michael J. "Pyramids to Fall." *New Mexico Daily Lobo,* 30 July 1987: 27.

Gardner, Marilyn. "Ms. Magazine at 15: Issues Change, Not Theme." *Albuquerque Journal,* 27 July 1987: B3.

Gelfand, M. Howard. "Parkettes Today, But Lewdafisks Tomorrow?" *MPLS* (Minneapolis) 6 (Oct. 1978): 4.

Glicksberg, Charles I. "Extracurricular Activities and School Morale." *American School Board Journal* 110 (May 1945): 36-37.

Gonzales, Arturo F., Jr. "The First College Cheer." *American Mercury* 83 (Nov. 1956): 101-04.

Goodger, John. "Ritual Solidarity and Sport." *Acta Sociologica* (Norway) 29 (1986): 219-24.

Goodman, C.E. "Unusual Nerve Injuries in Recreational Activities." *American Journal of Sports Medicine* 11 (July/Aug. 1983): 224-27.

Gran, Susie. "Club, Private Company Offer APS Pay-for-Play After-school Programs." *Albuquerque Tribune,* 27 Apr. 1990: A1.

Grizzard, Lewis. "Are You a Bimbo? Does Your Name End in 'i'?" *Albuquerque Tribune,* 13 Oct. 1987: C2.

Hainfeld, Harold. "Cheerleading in Grade and Junior High." *School Activities* 30 (Dec. 1958): 116-17.

Hatton, Charles Thomas, and Robert W. Hatton. "The Sideline Show." *Journal of the National Association for Women Deans, Administrators, and Counselors* 42 (Fall 1978): 23-28.

Henderson, Lana. "Cowboys Cheerleaders Building an Industry on the Dallas Woman." *Dallas Magazine* 57 (Sept. 1978): 18.

"High-school Cheerleaders: Agile Trio at Whiting, Ind., Specialize in Rhythm-nastics." *Life* 11 (10 Nov. 1941): 58-60.

Hinson, Hal. "New on Video." *Washington Post,* 24 Dec. 1992: C7.

Hoest, Bunny, and John Reiner. "Laugh Parade," cartoon. *Parade Magazine,* 21 June 1992: 12.

Hollander, Nicole. "Sylvia," comic strip. *Arlington (VA) Journal,* 24 June 1992: D3.

Hoosiers, 35 mm, 114 mins., Orion, 1987.

"The 'In' Crowd." *Self* Vol. 15 (Oct. 1993): 48.

Ivins, Molly. "As Thousands Cheer." *Progressive* 53 (Aug. 1989): 35.

Iyer, Pico. "In California: Catching the Spirit." *Time* 126 (12 Aug. 1985): 8.

Johnston, Lynn. "For Better or For Worse," comic strip. *Albuquerque Tribune,* 30 Jan. 1990: D6.

Joseph, Nathan, and Nicholas Alex. "The Uniform: A Sociological Perspective." *American Journal of Sociology* 77 (Jan. 1972): 719-30.

"Judi Hamrick To Be Bride of Gregg Underwood." *Washington Post,* 18 Oct. 1989: B7.

"Judson, Churchill Cheerleaders Capture Honors at National Competition." *San Antonio (TX) Express-News,* 30 Dec. 1992: 3B

Kaemper, Mike. "Cheerleaders Won't Be Tested For Drugs." *New Mexico Daily Lobo,* 2 Feb. 1988: 1.

Kaplan, Janice. "Jeers For Cheerleaders." *Seventeen* 36 (Oct. 1977): 42.

Keefe, Mike. Editorial cartoon. *Fayetteville (NC) Observer,* 6 Aug. 1990: 14A.

Kempley, Rita. "Land of Dashed Dreams." *Washington Post,* 6 Feb. 1988: G5.

"Key to Cheerleading: 'Big, Strong, Definite' Motions." *New York Times,* 21 Sept. 1967: 54.

Keyes, Ralph. "Rah! Rah! What? They Didn't Make Cheerleader." *Cosmopolitan* 196 (Mar. 1984): 168.

Kirksey, Jim. "'Save the Pony Express' Campaign Begins." *Denver Post,* 4 Mar. 1980: 3.

Kirshenbaum, Jerry. "They Thought They Could . . . and They Did!" *Sports Illustrated* 60 (19 Mar. 1984): 18.

Klemesrud, Judy. "Still the Rah-Rah, But Some Aren't Cheering." *New York Times,* 11 Oct. 1971: 44.

Kuralt, Charles. "Those Good Old Cheers Gone By." *Reader's Digest* 117 (Sept. 1980): 54-55.

Kurman, George. "What Does Girls' Cheerleading Communicate?" *Journal of Popular Culture* 20 (Fall 1986): 57-63.

Kutz, F.B. "Cheerleading Rules, Desirable Traits and Qualifications." *School Activities* 26 (May 1955): 310.

Larkin, Bob. "21st YAFL Season About to Kick Off." *Albuquerque Journal,* 22 July 1987: C5.

Leavy, Walter. "NFL Cheerleaders." *Ebony* 37 (Dec. 1981): 124.

Lee, James Ward. "Legends in Their Own Time: The Dallas Cowboy [*sic*] Cheerleaders." In *Legendary Ladies of Texas,* Francis Edward Abernethy, ed., 194-201. Publications of the Texas Folklore Society 43 (1981).

Leggett, Jim. "The Girl-Next-Door You Love To Have For Breakfast." *Star,* 28 May 1991: 16.

"Let Us Sigh For the Silenced Yell." *Literary Digest* 112 (2 Jan. 1932): 36.

"Let's Hear It For Pep Squad Beauty." *Teen* 27 (Sept. 1983): 94-95.

Livingston, Bob. "School Personnel Rehired." (*Mt. Carmel, IL*) *Daily Republican Register,* 19 Mar. 1991: 1.

——. "Cheerleader Selection Discussed." (*Mt. Carmel, IL*) *Daily Republican Register*, 24 Apr. 1991: 1.

Lopez, Greg. "You Don't Have To Hear To Cheer." *(Denver) Rocky Mountain News*, 31 Jan. 1993: 10-12.

Louthan, John. "Briefcase," cartoon. *Albuquerque Tribune*, 21 Mar. 1988: C4.

Lucas, 35 mm, 100 mins., 20th Century Fox, 1986.

Lundholm, Jean K., and John M. Littrell. "Desire for Thinness Among High-school Cheerleaders: Relationship to Disordered Eating and Weight Control Behavior." *Adolescence* 21 (Fall 1986): 573-79.

Lynch, Ron. "That's the Spirit!" *Seventeen* 44 (Aug. 1985): 352-57.

Malich, Suzanne. "Skate Firms Put Wheels On the Line." *Albuquerque Journal*, 9 Oct. 1988: D5.

Marston, Cathy. "Cheerleaders Display New Image, Organization." *Trinitonian*, Trinity University (San Antonio), 8 Sept. 1989: 3.

McHenry, Monica Ann, and Alan R. Reich. "Effective Airway Resistance and Vocal Sound Pressure Level in Cheerleaders With a History of Dysphonic Episodes." *Folia Phoniatrica* 37 (1985): 223-31.

"Miami Dolphin Cheerleaders Model 'Love Me, Read To Me' T-shirts." *American Libraries* 20 (Feb. 1989): 105.

Minton, Lynn. "Fresh Voices." *Parade Magazine*, 4 Oct. 1992: 26.

Mirage (San Antonio: Trinity University, 1923): 78; (1925): 124; (1929): 122; (1936): 60; (1938): 55; (1939): 90.

"Mom Pleads Innocent in Hitman Case." *Albuquerque Journal*, 1 Mar. 1991: A2.

Morrow, Lissa Megan. "38 . . . 24 . . . 36 . . . Hike!" *Los Angeles* 25 (Nov. 1980): 130.

Moss, Gary. "Fort Bragg Schools Plan Sports Teams." *Fayetteville (NC) Observer*, 29 Aug. 1989.

"Mr. Cheerleader." *American Magazine* 161 (Mar. 1956): 47.

Nathanson, Rick. "Ex-Eldorado Cheerleader Now Works For Pro Team." *Albuquerque Journal*, 23 Aug. 1988: B1, B7.

"The NBA." *Albuquerque Tribune*, 28 Nov. 1991: C4.

Nelson, Kate, and Hank Stuever. "Tuition Hike Won't Alter UNM Bottom-of-Barrel Salary Stance." *Albuquerque Tribune*, 16 Apr. 1991: A5.

"The New Faces of School Spirit." *UCLA Magazine* 2 (Summer 1990): 71.

Newman, Bruce. "Gimme an 'S,' Gimme an 'E,' Gimme . . . : Cheerleaders For Pro Football Teams." *Sports Illustrated* 48 (22 May 1978): 18-19.

——. "Eight Beauties and a Beat." *Sports Illustrated* 54 (16 Mar. 1981): 30-35.

"N.F.L.: The Nubile Female League?" *Women's Sports* 1 (Feb. 1979): 12.

Nilles, Virginia. "Cheerleading." *New York State Education* 42 (Mar. 1955): 392-93.

"No Kidding? Facts About Some Famous Folks." *Albuquerque Tribune,* 5 Aug. 1991: A2.

"November Yells That Win Games." *Literary Digest* 83 (8 Nov. 1924): 34-40.

Olcott, S. "Year-round Checklist For the Cheerleading Advisor: Part 1." *Scholastic Coach* 47 (Jan. 1978): 104, 130-31.

——. "Year-round Checklist For the Cheerleading Advisor: Part 2." *Scholastic Coach* 47 (Feb. 1978): 91, 130-31.

"Organized Cheering." *The Nation* 92 (5 Jan. 1911): 5-6.

Osborne, Linda Barrett. "Novel Reading." *Washington Post Book World,* 6 Jan. 1991: 8.

"Owner of 3 Companies Is Leading in Cheers." *New York Times,* 28 Oct. 1972: 39, 45.

Paine, Ralph D. "The Spirit of School and College Sport in English and American Football." *Century* 71 (Nov. 1905): 99-116.

Parsons, Dana. "Cheerleaders Lose Uniforms." *Denver Post,* 21 Nov. 1979: 2.

——. "TD's Loss Becomes Playboy Readers' Gain." *Denver Post,* 25 Nov. 1979: 2.

——. "Petitions 'Won't Change' Pony Express Decision." *Denver Post,* 5 Mar. 1980: 20.

——. "Ex-Pony Express Members Still Reliving Daze of Noise, Glamour." *Denver Post,* 2 Nov. 1980: 24.

"Paula Abdul Tops MTV Awards as 'Straight Up' Wins 4 Times." *Fayetteville (NC) Observer,* 7 Sept. 1989.

"Paulette Marie Howell," obituary. *Washington Post,* 28 Dec. 1990: F4.

Payne, Henry. Editorial cartoon. *Albuquerque Tribune,* 20 Oct. 1987: A6.

Peele, Rodney. "Wakefield Cheerleaders Top County." *(Arlington, VA) Sun Weekly,* 22 Nov. 1994: 5.

"Peptalk: Let's Hear It For Spirit!" *Teen* 28 (June 1984): 64.

Peterson, Anne M. "Emmy-winning, Double-platinum Paula Abdul Has an Itch to Act." *Albuquerque Tribune,* 27 Nov. 1989: B7.

Petty, Rachel. Letter to the Editor. *Albuquerque Tribune,* 30 Apr. 1990: A6.

The Pom Pom Girls, 35 mm, 90 mins., Crown International, 1976.

"Pregnant Cheerleaders Raise Fuss." *San Antonio (TX) Express-News,* 10 Oct. 1993: 1D.

Pressley, Sue Anne. "Texas Steel, Senate-Ready." *Washington Post,* 14 June 1993: D1.

"Program Scheduled For Cheerleaders." *New York Times*, 9 June 1974: NJ 35.

Promised Land, 35 mm, 100 mins., Vestron Pictures, 1987.

Quindlen, Anna. "Little League's Lot Better Now When Pitcher's a Girl." *Albuquerque Tribune*, 28 June 1988: D2.

Radcliffe, Donnie. "Festivities Fit For a Queen: Pomp & Circumstance Aplenty For Elizabeth II's Visit." *Washington Post*, 13 May 1991: B8

Ralston, Jeannie. "Rah! Power." *Texas Monthly* 22 (Oct. 1994): 150-55.

"Razzle-dazzle; CBS Football Coverage." *Newsweek* 64 (28 Sept. 1964): 65.

Reck, Franklin M. "All Aboard the Pep Special!" *World Review* 7 (15 Oct. 1928): 74-75.

Reid, William A. Letter to Sports Editor. *Albuquerque Tribune*, 2 June 1989: C10.

Roessner, Barbara. "Are Cheerleaders on the Way Out?" Reprinted from the *Hartford Courant* in *This World*, 1 Oct. 1989: 3.

Rottkov, Richard. "The Great NASL Cheerleader Explosion: Boon or Bust?" *Soccer* 5 (Apr.-May 1979): 17.

——. "The Making of a Cosmos Girl 1979." *Soccer* 5 (Apr.-May 1979): 20.

Ryan, Michael. "Here, Everybody Gets To Play." *Parade Magazine*, 15 Mar. 1992: 10.

Ryan, Pat. "Once It Was Only Sis-boom-bah! Collegiate Cheerleaders." *Sports Illustrated* 30 (6 Jan. 1969): 44-55.

Salazar, Carlos. "Ex-cheerleader, Teacher 'Grego' Pino Dies at 58." *Albuquerque Tribune*, 13 July 1989: D2.

Salter, Stephanie. "There's Gold in Them Nuggets: 49ers Promotional Singing and Dancing Group." *Sports Illustrated* 41 (23 Sept. 1974): 38-42.

Samson, John K. "Cheers For Best: Bernalillo Cheerleaders Have Eyes on Nationals." *Albuquerque Tribune*, 9 Feb. 1989: B1, B4.

Schafer, Ed. "Former Poet Laureate Dies of Cancer at 71." *Albuquerque Journal*, 7 July 1991: E16.

Secrest, Tracey. "Competing Cheerleaders?" *York (PA) Sunday News*, 2 Dec. 1990: A6.

"Select Rally Squad on Sound Basis." *School Activities* 30 (Sept. 1958): 37.

Seligson, Tom. "The Truth About Jane Pauley." *Parade Magazine*, 20 Sept. 1987: 4-7.

"Sex In the Locker Room, and on the Football Field Fuels Old Controversy." *Jet* 55 (19 Oct. 1978): 46.

Shah, Diane K. "Sis-Boom-Bah!" *Newsweek* 90 (7 Nov. 1977): 87.

"The She on Prep Cheerleading Squad Was a 26-year-old He." *Albuquerque Tribune*, 20 Sept. 1990: A4.

Shields, R.W., and I.B. Jacobs. "Median Palmer Digital Neuropathy in a Cheerleader." *Archives of Physical Medicine and Rehabilitation* 67 (Nov. 1986): 824-26.

Shister, Gail. "The Pro Football Cheerleaders: What They're Like, How Much They Make, How They Feel About All That Shake, Shake, Shake They Do." *Glamour* 79 (Feb. 1981): 166.

Shoenstein, Ralph C. "Fight, Fight, Fight in Moderation." *Saturday Evening Post* 248 (Oct. 1976): 62-63.

Shrake, Edwin. "Trouping the Colors For Gussie Nell Davis; Kilgore Rangerettes, College Dance-Drill Team." *Sports Illustrated* 41 (16 Dec. 1974): 44.

"Sis, Boom, Ah! Short History of the Art of Cheering." *Scholastic* 32 (12 Mar. 1938): 29.

Smith, Cathy. "The Cheer Career." *San Antonio (TX) Express-News Magazine*, 29 Sept. 1991: 17.

Sojka, Gregory S. "Evolution of the Student-Athlete in America."*Journal of Popular Culture* 16 (Spring 1983): 54-67.

"Some Names." *New Yorker* 59 (12 Dec. 1983): 46-47.

Spano, John. "School Gives Her Nothing To Cheer About." *Los Angeles Times*, 23 Oct. 1986: II 1, 5.

"Spry Gals' Giant Leap." *Life* 47 (2 Nov. 1959): 59.

"'Stage Mom' Gets 15 Years For Death Plot." *Albuquerque Tribune*, 5 Sept. 1991: C3.

Staples, M.L. "School Morale Through the Pep Assembly." *School Activities* 11 (Sept. 1939): 17-18.

Stark, Grace W. "Fun in College." *Peabody Journal of Education* 21 (Mar. 1944): 269-74.

"State Cheerleading: Local Schools Earn Top Prizes." *Albuquerque Tribune*, 8 Apr. 1991: B3.

Steptoe, Sonja. "The Pom-pom Chronicles." *Sports Illustrated* 75 (6 Jan. 1992): 40-44.

Stevens, Richard. "Madhouse Football: Young America Football League Needs Bigger Place To Play." *Albuquerque Tribune*, 28 Oct. 1991: F6.

Suarez, Leo. "A Conflict of Interest?" *Sporting News* 202 (3 Nov. 1986): 36.

"Susie Walker Is First Couger in the NFL." *(Kutztown, PA) Patriot*, 27 Dec. 1990: 1, 7.

Swatos, William H., Jr. "On Being Virgin: Theories and Data." *International Journal of Women's Studies* 4 (Nov.-Dec. 1981): 517-26.

Tall Story, 35 mm, 89 mins., Warner Bros., 1960.

"Teen Births Stir Debate on Policies: Youths Account For 25% of All U.S. Abortions." *Albuquerque Journal*, 8 Nov. 1987: B1.

Tehranzadeh, Jamshid, David A. Labosky, and Orlando F. Gabriele. "Ganglion Cysts and Tear of Triangular Fibrocartilages of Both Wrists in a Cheerleader." *American Journal of Sports Medicine* 11 (Sept./Oct. 1983): 357-59.

"Texas 'Cheerleader Mom' To Get New Murder-for-hire Trial." *Albuquerque Tribune*, 14 Oct. 1994: A4.

"They Don't Boo; Do You? Pepnocrats of Connersville, Ind. High School." *Scholastic* 31 (13 Nov. 1937): 31.

"3 Ex-Oiler Cheerleaders Sue Team For $23.5 Million." *Jet* 69 (21 Oct. 1985): 47.

Timson, Judith. "Bounce For Glory; Canadian Football League Cheerleaders." *Maclean's* 91 (21 Aug. 1978): 29-32.

Troidl, Robert, and Sarah Peterson. "Mesa Public Schools: As Seen Through the Eyes of 1982-83 Seniors." ERIC, ED 249236 (1983), Abstract.

"U. of Miss. Still Working To Drop Confederate Flag." *Chronicle of Higher Education*, 10 July 1991: A3.

Universal Partner Stunts for Cheerleading, video. Memphis: Universal Cheerleaders Association, 1984.

Universal Tumbling For Cheerleading, video. Memphis: Universal Cheerleaders Association, 1984.

"The University of Connecticut Has Dropped Its Weight Limit For Female Cheerleaders." *Chronicle of Higher Education*, 4 Sept. 1991: A45.

Vecsey, George. "Young Footballers Getting Ready Too." *New York Times*, 21 Aug. 1973: 34.

Webb, Greg. "Cheerleaders—Spirit Leaders and Then Some!" *Interscholastic Athletic Administration* 11 (Fall 1984): 18-19.

Weber, Larry J., and others. "Factors Related to Exclusion of Students From School Activities." ERIC, ED 204837 (1981), Abstract.

Weinraub, Judith. "Redskinettes See Red: Nepotism, Racism Alleged; Tryout To Be Boycotted." *Washington Post*, 22 Mar. 1990: C2.

——. "The Revolt of the Redskinettes." *Washington Post*, 20 Sept. 1992: F1, F6.

Wieder, Robert. "The First Hurrah: The Oakland Invaders Get a Cheerleading Squad—and How." *California Magazine* 8 (Apr. 1983): 68.

"Willing To Kill." *Washington Post*, 7 Nov. 1992: G5.

Wiscombe, Janet. "Smiles Don't Express a Big Happy Family." *Denver Post*, 22 Nov. 1979: 51, 56.

"With Gusto: Cheerleaders from St. Joseph by the Sea High School Competing in the Fifth Annual Cheerleading Contest of the New

York Catholic Youth Organizations." *New York Times*, 26 Feb. 1973: 35.

Wolkomir, Richard. "American Sign Language: 'It's Not Mouth Stuff—It's Brain Stuff.'" *Smithsonian* 23 (July 1992): 30-41.

"Women's Lib Rah! Rah!" *New York Times*, 19 Jan. 1975: 103.

"The Yell-Leader: An American Functionary." *Times* (London) *Educational Supplement* 755 (19 Oct. 1929): 456.

Yodice, James. "Exodus From Mountainair Changed Football Forever." *Albuquerque Journal*, 16 Oct. 1988: E1, E5.

Zingelman, Joan. Letter to the Editor. *Denver Post*, 4 Mar. 1980: 15.

Index

163